Census of Great Britain, 1851. Educat Britain, the official report of H. Mann and Horace Mann

Publisher's Note

The book descriptions we ask booksellers to display prominently warn that this is an historic book with numerous typos or missing text; it is not indexed or illustrated.

The book was created using optical character recognition software. The software is 99 percent accurate if the book is in good condition. However, we do understand that even one percent can be an annoying number of typos! And sometimes all or part of a page may be missing from our copy of the book. Or the paper may be so discolored from age that it is difficult to read. We apologize and gratefully acknowledge Google's assistance.

After we re-typeset and design a book, the page numbers change so the old index and table of contents no longer work. Therefore, we often remove them; otherwise, please ignore them.

Our books sell so few copies that you would have to pay hundreds of dollars to cover the cost of our proof reading and fixing the typos, missing text and index. Instead we let most customers download a free copy of the original typo-free scanned book. Simply enter the barcode number from the back cover of the paperback in the Free Book form at www.RareBooksClub.com. You may also qualify for a free trial membership in our book club to download up to four books for free. Simply enter the barcode number from the back cover onto the membership form on our home page. The book club entitles you to select from more than a million books at no additional charge. Simply enter the title or subject onto the search form to find the books.

If you have any questions, could you please be so kind as to consult our Frequently Asked Questions page at www.RareBooksClub.com/faqs.cfm? You are also welcome to contact us there.
General Books LLC™, Memphis, USA, 2012.

❈ ❈ ❈ ❈ ❈ ❈ ❈ ❈

by Authority Of The Registrar General.
CENSUS OF GREAT BRITAIN, 1851.
EDUCATION IN GREAT BRITAIN. BEING THE OFFICIAL REPORT OF HORACE MANN,
Of Lincoln's Inn, Esq., Bajikisteh-at-law,
To
George Graham, Esq., Registrar-General; WITH SELECTED TABLES.
by Authority Of The Registrar-general.
CENSUS OP GREAT BRITAIN, 1851.
EDUCATION
IN
GREAT BRITAIN.
BEING
THE OFFICIAL REPORT
OF
HORACE MANN,
Of Lincoln's Inn, Esq., Barrister-At-Law,
TO
George Graham, Esq., Registrar-General;
WITH SELECTED TABLES.
CONTENTS.
EDUCATION IN ENGLAND AND WALES:— Page
Letter from the Registrar General to Viscount Palmerston--7—8
REPORT:—
Report from Mr. Horace Mann to the Registrar General:—
Difficulties encountered in prosecuting the inquiry-9
Summary result---... 10
Whether this result is satisfactory depends on three questions,
viz., 1. Is the number of scholars *increasing?* 2. Is the *present* number adequate? 3. Is the present number well instructed?-11
1. Progress of popular education in England... 11—16
2. Actual amount (numerically) of day school education as compared with the amount required-17—26
3. Quality of existing instruction in day schools--27—31
Number of children who *might* be in day schools---32—33
Causes why so many are *not* in day schools---34—37
Remedies proposed...... 37—38
What are the means and agencies by which education is to be extended 39
View of *existing* educational agencies:
Primary Education:
1. *Day Schools:*
Private Day Schools-4.0—41
Public Day Schools-.--. 41—63
2. *Evening Schools for Children* ...-63
Secondary Education:
1. *Evening Schools for Adults* ...-64—65
2. *Literary, Scientific, and Mechanics' Institutions*-66
Sunday Schools.... 67—74
Present aspect of educational parties-----75—83
Collateral means of promoting popular education--85
SUMMARY TABLES:
Table A.—Day Schools, Sunday Schools, and Evening Schools for
Adults. *(Summary of England and Wales)*-90
Table B.—Day Schools, classified according to the sources of their maintenance. *(Summary of England and Wales)*--91
Supplement I. to Table B.—Number of Schools which,
supported principally by Endowments, are partly also
maintained by Subscriptions of Religious Bodies-92
Supplement II. to Table B.—Total of Schools supported
in *any degree* by Religious Bodies.... 92

Supplement III. to Table B.—Number of Schools which,
supported principally by Subscriptions of Religious Bodies,
are partly also maintained by Endowments--93

Table C.—*Income* of Public Day Schools, and the sources of Income 94

Table D.—Number of Schools having Endowments of particular amounts--------96

Table E.—Number of *Teachers* in Public Schools; distinguishing adult from juvenile Teachers-----97

Table P.—*Course of Instruction* in Public Day Schools--98

Table G.— Do. in Public and Private Day Schools 100

SUMMARY TABLES—*continued.* Page

Table H.—*Ages* of Scholars in quinquennial periods--101

Table I.—*Dates* at which existing Day Schools were established; distinguishing Public from Private Schools; and showing each county.....-102

Table K.—*Dates* at which existing Public Day Schools were established; distinguishing each class of Schools---104

Table L.—Number of Scholars *attending* compared with the number *on the books* in each of the various classes of Day Schools. (Two counties, Lancashire and Lincolnshire)---106

Table M.—Comparison between the ages of Scholars in Public Day Schools, the ages of those in Private Day Schools. (Two counties, Lancashire and Lincolnshire)....-107

Table N.—Average annual *Remuneration of Teachers* in Public Day Schools; distinguishing the various classes of Schools. (Two counties, Lancashire and Lincolnshire)---108

Table O.—Day Schools, classified according to their sources of maintenance. (In *Counties*) ----110

Table P.—Day Schools, classified according to their sources of maintenance. (In forty-five of the principal *Boroughs and Large* 125 *Towns'*) ...--

Table Q Number of Sunday Schools and Scholars, distinguishing the number belonging to each Religious Body... 137

Table R.—The same particulars as to each of forty-five of the principal *Boroughs* and *Large Towns* ---- 138

Table S.—Evening Schools for Adults--... 144

Table T.—Subjects taught in Evening Schools for Adults--146

Table U.—Occupations of Adult Evening Scholars---148

Illustrative Tables...... 150

EDUCATION IN SCOTLAND:—

Report from Mr. Horace Mann to the Registrar-General--153

Table A.—Day Schools, classified according to their sources of maintenance....... 158

Table B.—Sabbath Schools, classified according to the Religious Denominations which support them-----157

Supplement I. to Table A., showing the number of Schools supported in *any degree* by Endowments---158

Supplement n. to Table A., showing the number of Schools supported in *any degree* by Religious Bodies-158

Table C.—Income of Public Day Schools----159

Table D.—Course of Instruction in Public and Private Day Schools 160

Table E.—Number of Scholars instructed in various branches of learning--------162

Table E.—Number of Teachers in Public Schools---164

Table G.—Remuneration of Teachers in Public Schools--165

Table H.—Dates at which existing Public Schools were established-166

Table I Classified view of existing Public Schools... 168

Table K Showing the ages of Scholars in quinquennial Periods-169

Table L.—Endowment of Public Schools----170

Table M.—Sabbath Schools and Teachers, specified according to the Denominations which support them----171

Table N.—Dates at which existing Sabbath Schools were established 172

Appendix:—Explanatory Notes as to the mode of procuring and digesting the Returns------173

PREFACE.

Popular Education is now of so much interest to all classes and parties in this country, that it is highly essential to place within the reach of the public generally authentic information upon the subject. By the agency of that great national undertaking — the Census — a more full and accurate inquiry into the educational condition of Great Britain has been accomplished than any previously attempted; and it will be admitted that the results are too valuable to be confined within the limited circulation of an official publication, of which but few copies are printed besides those designed for the use of members of the Legislature and other public personages. At a time when the various questions connected with this subject give rise to much discussion, the important statistics contained in the Educational Census cannot fail to be extremely useful—indeed, almost indispensable—to all who desire to form their judgment upon facts. To such the present abridgment of the official Abstract will be acceptable. It contains, besides all the most important Tables, the whole of the Report of Mr. Horace Mann, to whom the duty of digesting the returns was confided, and who has brought out the principal results with so much ability and impartiality that it has been.deemed proper to give his Report without curtailment. To render the information more complete, the general results of the inquiry in Scotland are also given.

The success of the abridgment recently issued of the "Census of Religious Worship," of which twenty-one thousand copies have already been sold, justifies the belief that the present publication, designed to furnish to all classes facts, not of an ephemeral character, but of great and permanent interest, will meet with encouragement. The Registrar General, Major Graham, whose desire it is to render the official returns of the Census available for *popular* information, and who gave the previous publication the sanction of his approval, has also kindly allowed the Editor of the present work to send it forth with his express authority.

London, 10th June 1854.

ut ENGLAND AND WALES. TO THE RIGHT HON. THE VISCOUNT PALMERSTON, M. P., G.C.B., HER MAJESTY'S SECRETARY OF STATE FOR

THE HOME DEPARTMENT.

My Lord, Census Office, 31st March 1854.

I Have the honour to transmit to your Lordship, in order that they may be laid before both Houses of Parliament, the accompanying Tables relating to the existing Educational Establishments in England and Wales, and the number of Scholars under instruction.

Similar returns have been presented to Parliament with respect to Scotland and the Islands in the British Seas.

Tables also have been presented showing the accommodation afforded by the various Churches and other Places of Public Religious Worship throughout Great Britain, and the number of persons frequenting them.

I regret the delay which has occurred in completing these returns; but it must be borne in mind that in this office at the same time Tables were being prepared showing the Number, Sex, Age, Occupation, Civil Condition, and Birthplace of Twenty-one Millions of People, with their distribution over the face of the country; the number of Houses and the extent of Acreage in every Parish; the numbers in the Army, Royal Navy, and Merchant Service at home and abroad; the number of Blind and of Deaf and Dumb; the number of inmates of Workhouses, Gaols, and other public Institutions; the number of Acres cultivated and of Men employed by Farmers; and other particulars.

I suggested that, at the time of taking the Census, inquiries into Religion and Education should be instituted; because it appeared to me that, the country being divided for the particular purpose of ascertaining the numbers of the people into nearly 40,000 Districts, each having its special paid Enumerator, it wa3 desirable to embrace that opportunity, which would not again occur for ten years, to obtain, without additional expense, information upon two subjects to which the attention of the public is much directed.

The public now know the number of Places of Public Religious Worship belonging to the Established Church and to the several Denominations, with the number of Sittings — distinguishing free from appropriated — the different periods of the day at which they are open — and also the number of attendants on 30th March 1851.

They are also informed of the date at which the different buildings were erected; the amount of accommodation in large towns as compared with the rest of the country; the places provided with the greatest and the least amount of accommodation; the position of the Church of England and the Dissenting Bodies in different parts of England; and other similar information.

The subject not having been previously investigated, the information was of a novel character. The Report and the Tables were prepared, by Mr. Horace Mann with much ability; and the interest taken in them by the public has been very great, for more than 20,000 copies have been already sold of an abridged edition.

In like manner I hope that the Tables now transmitted to your Lordship, referring to the Education of the people, will not be considered devoid of interest.

The public will probably be glad to know the number of children to whom education is now afforded, compared with the number of scholars at former periods when a similar investigation was attempted, the number of Day Schools, and the number of scholars on the books of each school compared with the actual number in attendance on 31st March 1851, in each County, and in each large town in England and Wales; the income of the schools, and the sources from which it is obtained; the quality of instruction given; the number of teachers, distinguishing adults; the remuneration of teachers in public schools; the ages of the scholars; the dates at which the schools were established; and the number of schools of each distinct class, as National, British, Ragged, &c. &c.

Similar information is given as to Sunday Schools; and for each county is stated the number of Evening Schools for adults—the period during which they are open—together with the number of scholars, their occupation, and the amount of their payments, and the course of instruction imparted to them.

Great pains have been taken to obtain as complete returns as is possible. Still they cannot be stated to be entirely perfect—indeed I know of few statistical tables of which that can be said with entire truth—but I believe that in considering the question of providing education for the people these returns may be relied upon for all practical purposes.

I rejoice that in 1851 Her Majesty's Government adhered to their determination to endeavour to ascertain these particulars, notwithstanding the appeals which were in some instances made to them to abandon the project, on the plea that the proposed inquiries were too minute and inquisitorial—that they were so numerous that the expense of the Census would be increased, and that the returns would draw an invidious distinction between the Church of England and Dissenters—and notwithstanding the announcement from some persons in authority that they would use such power as they possessed to induce those whom they could influence not to pay any attention to the queries, but to leave them unanswered.

Mr. Horace Mann has, under my superintendence, chiefly conducted these inquiries; and I hope that your Lordship will think that he has with good judgment and ability performed the task thus confided to him.

, I have the honour to be, MyTLord, Your faithful Servant,

GEOEGE GRAHAM,

Registrar-General.

REPORT. 10 GEORGE GRAHAM, Esq. *$c. $c. Sfc.* REGISTRAR-GENERAL OF BIRTHS, DEATHS, AND MARRIAGES.

Sir,

4 • Census of Great Britain, 1851. Education in Great Britain, the official report of H. Mann • Census office and Horace Mann

I Have now the honor to lay before you the tabulated results of the inquiry undertaken, in pursuance of your directions, as a part of the decennial Census, with respect to the existing educational provision in this country.

The interval will probably appear considerable which has elapsed between Difficulties enthe collection of the returns and the present publication of results. The cause posecuting" of this delay is to be found in the peculiar circumstances under which the inquiry. investigation was conducted. The opposition which the scheme encountered in some quarters, led to the discovery that inquiries on this subject did not strictly come within the scope of the Census Act, and could not therefore be assisted by the compulsory provisions which secured complete and truthful answers to the ordinary questions as to Age, Condition, Occupation, Birthplace, &c. As the authoritative interpretation, in this sense, of an ambiguous section of the Act was not expressed till just upon the eve of the Census, when the whole of the arrangements had been settled and the necessary forms despatched to every corner of Great Britain, it appeared to you that, rather than give up all chance of some result from the extensive preparations which had been matured, it would be better to continue the inquiry on a purely *voluntary* basis—intimating to the heads of schools that they were not *compellable to* fill up the returns, and that their own opinion of the value of an accurate Census of Education was the only influence by which they were expected to be guided. This was the course pursued; and the 30,610 Enumerators delivered schedules of questions to upwards of 70,000 heads of schools. "When, in the course of May 1851,these schedules were returned to the Census office, together with the Enumerators' Lists of Schools, it was perceived that, while from the vast majority of schools returns had been supplied, there yet remained a considerable number with respect to which—either from indifference of the Census officers on a matter which had been confessed to be not strictly within the Act, or from unwillingness on the part of school authorities—no information had been given. The question then arose, whether, as so much valuable information had been positively gathered, and as the deficiency, though in itself considerable, was small compared with what had been accomplished, any effort should be made to give completeness to the inquiry by a further application to those schools concerning which intelligence was needed. Your conclusion was, that though, the inquiry, undertaken mainly on y .r own responsibility—it would not be proper to divert for such a purpose a. y considerable portion of the strength required for an expeditious digest of the more immediate subject-matter of the Census; yet, as far as was consistent with the latter object, it would be decidedly expedient to make renewed exertions to render these returns, if not complete, at all events so full as to approach completeness, and to yield important information on a subject occupying much of the attention of the public, and apparently about to occupy the notice of the Parliament. Accordingly, a correspondence was opened with the Census officers with respect to several thousands of schools. Not less than a year elapsed before this correspondence closed; but at its termination it became apparent that the information which had been collected with so much trouble, was, though still to some extent deficient, so extensive as to give by far the amplest view attainable of our educational position—indeed, sufficiently extensive to determine many of the problems recently the subjects of much controversy. Upon ascertaining this unlooked-for completeness, you determined to conduct the tabulation of the facts in a more elaborate manner than was at first designed; and the interval from then till now has been found necessary for the task of producing the facts in their present aspect—an interval made necessary not only by the urgent demands of the other departments of the Census, but also by the multiplicity and complexity of the particulars contained in the educational returns.

Stated summarily, the result of the inquiry is, that returns have been received from 44,836 day schools (15,411 public and 29,425 private); from 23,137 Sunday schools; from 1,545 evening schools for adults; and from 1,057 Literary, Scientific, and Mechanics' Institutions. But in addition to the above number of schools, from which returns were received, the lists supplied by the enumerators make mention of 1,206 other day schools (107 public and 1,099 private) and 377 other Sunday schools, from which *no* returns were procurable. If we assume that each of these last-named schools contained, upon an average, as many scholars as did each of the schools which made returns, the ultimate result of the Educational Census will be this: f The term "school," throughout this publication, is used to denote a distinct *establishment.* Thus, a school for both boys and girls, if under one general management and conducted in one range of buildings, is regarded as only one school, although the tuition may be carried on in separate compartments of the building, under separate superintendence.

t This view presents the state of things as shown by the information which has reached the Census Office through the instrumentality of the enumerators. It is unquestionably an under statement of existing means of education; sine no doubt a certain number of schools were not enumerated by these officers. My own impression is, that the number of scholars belonging to the various *Bay Schools* cannot be short of 2,200,000, and that the number of scholars on the books of the various *Sunday Schools* cannot be less than 2,500,000; but in all the general calculations in this Report the figures given above are used. X If it be assumed that the proportion of the *sexes* was the same in the schools which sent no returns as in those which sent returns, the total number of males in *Day Schools* would be 1,157,685, and of females 986,693; of which there would have been in *Public* Schools, 801,156 males and 621,826 females, and in *Private* Schools, 356,529 males and 364,867 females. On a similar assumption, the male scholars in *Sunday*

Scltools would have been 1,193,788, and the female scholars 1,213,854.

The answer to the question, "whether this statement shows our educational Is this result position to be satisfactory or not," depends upon the answers given to several factory? other questions; such as: 1st. Does the present state of education, as exhibited above, display considerable advance upon its state in former periods, so as to give evidence of *progress?* 2d. What number of children, out of the population of England and Wales in 1851, should constantly be found at school?—involving the questions of school age, duration of school attendance, &c.' 3d. What is the *character of the instruction* afforded to existing scholars?

1. *Progress of Popular Education in England.*

Popular education may be said to be almost entirely the creation of the Popular educapresent century. The records and the recollections which describe society so the presenTM recently as fifty years ago bear testimony to a state of ignorance and immorality centluTso dense and general that, if any member of the present generation could be suddenly transported to that earlier period, he would probably be scarcely able, notwithstanding many abiding landmarks, to believe himself in England, and would certainly regard the change which half a century has witnessed in the manners of the people as but little short of the miraculous. Comparison is scarcely possible between the groups of gambling, swearing children—no unfavourable example of young England then—whom Raikes of Gloucester, in 1781, with difficulty collected in the *first Sunday School,* and any single class of the 2,400,000 scholars who now gather with alacrity, and even with affection, round their 318,000 teachers. In contemplating the various agencies by which, throughout the intervening period, the habits of the people have been so conspicuously improved, it is of course impossible to assign to each its positive share of influence in accomplishing this change; but it may very safely be affirmed that no small portion of the happy transformation is attributable to the vast accession which has been effected in the number of our daily and Sunday schools.

The latter took precedence in the educational race. The work which the Sunday schools. Gloucester publisher originated rapidly advanced: Religious Bodies, more especially Dissenters, heartily embraced the plan; and the present century has seen the system so extended, that scarcely any regular place of worship now existing is without its Sunday school.

The same awakened sense of neighbourly responsibility which thus produced Day schools. the Sunday school, soon after gave a mighty impulse to the work of *daily* education. The *Popular Day School* epoch dates from 1796, when the youthful Quaker, Joseph Lancaster, began, in his father's house in Southwark, to instruct the children of the poor. Enthusiastic in his calling and benevolent to rashness in his disposition, he assumed towards his scholars more the character of Joseph Languardian than of master; easily remitting to the poorer children even the Britislfand 6 scanty pittance charged, and often furnishing with food the most distressed. gTM'P'Soho01 No wonder that his scholars multiplied with great rapidity: they numbered 90 ere he was 18 years old, and afterwards came pouring in upon him "like flocks of sheep," till in 1798 they reached as many as 1,000. In his perplexity how to provide sufficient teachers, he, according to his friends, invented; or, according to his enemies, derived from Dr. Bell, the plan of teaching younger children and economy procured for it extensive favour. Lancaster, absorbed in the idea of educating all the youth of Britain on this system, lectured through the land with great success—obtained the patronage of royalty—established schools— and raised considerable funds. But he was not the man to guide the movement which he had originated: ardent, visionary, destitute of worldly prudence, the very qualities which made him so successful as a teacher and a missionary in the cause of education rendered him incapable as an administrator. His affairs became embarrassed: he himself was tossed about through varied troubles, passing from a prison to prosperity, and then again reduced to bankruptcy; until, in 1818, he departed for America, where, after twenty years of suffering, brightened by some intervals of popularity but none of prudence, his life was terminated by an accident, in 1838, in the streets of New York. Ten years before he quitted England the development of his system was committed into abler hands; the prominent result of which proceeding was the foundation, in 1808, of "the British And Foreign School Society."

Dr. Bell and the In 1792, six years before the monitors of Lancaster began their labours, Society. the experiment of juvenile instructors was successfully commenced in India, where Dr. Bell, then Superintendent of the Military Orphan School, Madras, unable to induce the usher there to teach the younger children to write the alphabet in sand, was led to supersede him by a boy of eight years old, whose services proved so efficient, that the Doctor, generalizing from this instance, and considering the plan to be of almost universal application, ardently developed his idea, and on his return to England in 1796 urged warmly the adoption of his system as the most effectual means of rapidly extending popular instruction. Andrew Bell was the very opposite of Joseph Lancaster m all except a common enthusiasm for instruction on the 'mutual' or ' monitorial' system. A Scotchman (the son of a barber of Saint Andrew's), his career was just as much distinguished by invariable prudence as was Lancaster's by constant though benevolent improvidence. On leaving college in 1774, at the age of twentyone, Bell went to America, and spent his next live years as a tutor in Virginia, whence, in 1781, he returned to England, having suffered shipwreck on his passage. He now took orders in the English Church, and became the minister of the Episcopal Chapel at Leith. Applying for a Doctor's degree in Divinity, he received instead, from.the University of Saint

Andrew's, one in Medicine. In 1787 he sailed for India, where he was appointed chaplain to five or eix regiments. On the foundation of the Military Orphan Asylum, he became its honorary superintendent; and it was in this capacity that he made his experiment in' mutual instruction.' The result of this experiment he published, after his return to England in 1797, and made strenuous efforts to procure the general adoption of his scheme. In 1801 he became rector of Swanage, Dorsetshire; in 1808 the master of Sherborne Hospital; in 1818 a prebendary of Hereford Cathedral, and subsequently one of Westminster. He died in 1832, bequeathing his large fortune of 120,000/. principally to the Educational Institutions of his native country. It is, however, in connection with the National Society that Dr. Bell is chiefly known. The Lancasterian Schools have always been established on an unsectarian basis—no peculiar religious tenets being inculcated; the " Bible without note or comment" being the only religious school-book. Early in the history of these schools this plan appeared to many Churchmen unsatisfactory,—the distinctive doctrines of the Church of England being thus unrepresented; and a scheme was formed to organize, according to the new method, exclusively *Church* schools. This led to the The title of the Society, when formed in 1808, was " The Royal Lancasterian Institution for promoting the Education of the Children of the Poor." It received its present designation a few years amerwards.

establishment, in 1811, of the National Society For Promoting The Education Of The Poor In The Principles Of The Established Church.

The work of education now advanced with some rapidity; Lord Brougham Progress accombeing most conspicuous as the zealous champion of popular enlightenment. Bourns of 1818. The earliest statistics by which this progress may be measured are contained in the Parliamentary Returns of 1818. These, though defective, are sufficiently complete to show that a considerable step had then been taken towards a general instruction of the people. It appears that in that year the number of schools and scholars was as under:—

Nor did religious zeal, to which this great advance was almost wholly due, rest Further progress.

satisfied with this achievement. Fifteen years elapsed before another enumera- Returns of 1883. tion of schools was made; but this, when made, showed clearly that the interval had not been idly spent. Lord Kerry's Parliamentary Returns of 1833 were probably deficient by as much as 10 per cent.; but they suffice to prove a great increase of educational provision subsequent to 1818. This is the result:—

The population between 1818 and 1833 had increased by nearly 24 per cent., while during the same interval the number of Day scholars had increased by 89 per cent., and that of Sunday scholars by 225 per cent.f

Up to this period (1833) the whole of what had been accomplished in the Commencement work of popular education was the fruit of private liberality, incited mainly hfSd'of by religious zeal, and acting, in the matter of *daily* education, principally day schools, through the medium of the two great societies— the *British* and the *National.* But in 1833 the Government first proffered its assistance in the labour, and contributed till 1839 an annual grant of 20,00(W. Hitherto, upon the subject of National Education—the community nad been divided into two principal and two subordinate parties; the two primary consisting of the advocates and the opponents of popular instruction in the abstract—the two secondary being subdivisions of the former of these parties, and consisting, on the one hand, of In Liverpool alone, it was ascertained the omissions amounted to as many as 15,500 scholars; and though some few duplicate returns were made, there seems to be no doubt but that the omissions largely preponderated.

t These per-centages are of course subject to variation on account of the deficiencies in the two inquiries of 1818 and 1883, and on account of possible differences in the mode of enumerating the Scholars; but these variations cannot seriously diminish the rate of increase— still less can they affect the inference that a vast extension of Education was accomplished between these years. See some objections in a paper by Rev. C. Richson, M. A., read before the Man all those who thought that the Church of England, from her union with the State, was the sole legitimate instructress of the people, and should teach them in accordance with her special doctrines, and, upon the other hand, of all those who thought that the numerical position of seceders from the Church conferred on them a right to less dogmatic teaching—the whole Bible without any comment being the exclusive and sufficient standard. After the commencement of the Reform Bill epoch, the opponents of instruction for the million practically disappeared: the nation has been ever since almost unanimous in striving to extend to all the benefits of education, and till 1843 was almost equally unanimous in calling for the agency, in this direction, of the State in its central organified capacity. But no defined idea seems to have been prevalent of the mode in which the action of tne State should be exerted; and the Government, from 1833 to 1839—perplexed between the two great parties into which the friends of education were divided— could do nothing more than share the annual grant between the two great educational societies by which these parties then were represented. In 1839 and 1843, indeed, two measures were proposed by which it was intended to provide for a more immediate influence of the State: the former, the establishment of a Government Normal School—the latter, the education of children in factories; but the first of these was defeated by the opposition of the Church, and the second by the hostility of the Dissenters. It was thus made manifest that the decisive tendency of fifty years of private educational enterprise had been to bring the education of the people into such a close connection with religious bodies, that for any prudent Government it was impracticable either, on the one hand, to ignore the agency of these communities, or, on the other, in applying to educational purposes funds raised by general taxation, to recognifie the predominance of any particular section. Consequently the action of the Government has ever since been limited to a co-operation with religious bodies, so far as the latter have been willing to accept its aid; each grant being made conditional upon a previous voluntary contribution in a specified proportion to the grant. In 1839 the duty of administering these Parliamentary funds was transferred from the Treasury to the Committee of Privy Council on Education—not, however, without considerable opposition, on the ground of the supposed unconstitutional and irresponsible character of the suggested Board.

Simultaneously, the amount of the annual sum assigned for education was increased: from 1839 till 1841 inclusive, it was fixed at 30,000/; 40,000/. was allowed for 1842-3-4; and the augmentations subsequently have raised it up to *75,0001.* in 1845; 100,000/. in 1846 and 1847 J 125,000/. in 1848-9-50; 150,000/. in 1851-2; and 260,000/. in 1853.

The total amount of public money granted from 1833 to the end of 1850 was, as nearly as possible, 1,000,000/. ; and the portion *expended* in that interval was about 750,000/. None of this was given towards the expense of *maintaining* schools, but either towards the cost of *buildings*—for the purchase of school apparatus—or in aid of the salaries of efficient masters, mistresses, and teachers. Prior to 1847, however, no grants were made for any purposes except in aid of building schools and in aid of Normal schools. Part was appropriated to Scotland. Of the 500,000/. spent, between 1839-50, upon *English* schools, 405,000/. was contributed to schools connected with the Established Church; the other denominations receiving,—Wesleyans, 8,000/., and Roman Catholics, 1,049/. The British and Foreign School Society received 51,000/., and the Workhouse schools, 37,000/.

The account from which these figures are derived states the expenditure for the period between 1833 and the *8th of August* 1850. This probably presents the best view of the amount by which the schools returned in March 1851 arc likely to have been affected.—See "Education, National, Voluntary, and Free," by the late Joseph Fletcher, Esq., pp. 80,81.

In 1846 appeared the well-known Minutes which now form the basis of the present system of Government aid to Education.

Meanwhile, the State was not the only additional agent which appeared upon the scene. The effect of the abortive measure of 1843 (by which a certain predominance was intended to be given to the Church of England) was to foster in the minds of the Dissenters great suspicion and alarm respecting the designs and disposition of the Government towards them; and the Congregationalists and the Baptists—who had hitherto been strenuous advocates of State-interposition—losing, apparently, all hope that such interposition could be equitably managed, or without involving, contrary to their distinctive principles, the application of public money to religious teaching—felt themselves precluded from accepting any portion of the annual grants, exclaimed against the agency of Government altogether, and founded two societies of their own—the "congregational Board Of Education," and the "volunTary School Society." The establishment of these necessitated a secession from the "British and Foreign School Society;" but as the funds of that institution have not suffered, but increased, these new associations may be almost looked upon as *additional* agencies in the work of education, and as aiding to increase considerably the educational provision of the country. The Wesleyan Methodists, though equally, at first, suspicious of the Government, were not impelled to a denial of its right of interference altogether; and, indeed, have, since the adoption of a minute obviating some of their alarms, accepted Government assistance. Their exertions are, as those of the Congregationalists, *denominational;* and in the last ten years they have displayed remarkable activity. Most of the other religious bodies also have established Day Schools, more or less—the Roman Catholics especially. Indeed, no feature of our educational advancement in the present century is more remarkable than this,—the great extent to which whatever progress, satisfactory or otherwise, has been achieved, is owing to denominational activity or rivalry. This, doubtless, has been hitherto the most prevailing influence by which the cause of popular instruction has been aided. The most noticeable other movements tending to increase facilities for education are, the establishment in 1836 of the "Home And Colonial School Society," by which encouragement is given to. *Infant* education, and the *Ragged School* movement of more recent years by which a mighty stride has been accomplished towards the reclamation of those classes who most urgently require instruction, but who never would, in any other way, obtain it.—In the department of *Sunday Schools,* the chief encouragement was the formation of the Sunday School Union in 1803.

Having seen, then, what was the progress down to 1833—effected principally Present position in connexion with the *British* and the *National* Societies; and having indicated thTMKCd some of the additional agencies which have been put in operation since that time; the inquiry now occurs—what has been the result of this activity upon our *present* educational position? Dealing, as before, with totals only, it appears as to *Day Schools* that while in 1818 there was a scholar for every 17'25 persons, and in 1833 a scholar for every 11'27 persons, in 1851 there was a scholar for every 8"36 persons; and as to *Sunday Schools* it appears that while in 1818 there was one Sunday scholar for every 24 "40 persons, and in 1833 one scholar to every 9-28 persons, in 1851 there was one scholar to every 7'45 persons.f The increase between 1818 and 1851 was, of day scholars, 218 per cent., and of The'Congregationalists have raised, since 1843, about 160,0002. The Baptists mostly contribute to the Voluntary School Society.

t These calculations are given without any attempt (as none could be satisfactory) to allow for

Sunday scholars 404 per cent.; while the increase of population was but 54 per cent.

The following Table shows the figures for each of the three periods:

A further indication of the progress made in recent years in the work of educational provision is obtainable, to some extent, from a view of the *dates* at which existing Day Schools were founded or erected. The following statement shows how many of our present establishments had their origin in former and how many in later years.

As to *Private* Day Schools, indeed, the statement proves but little; since the frequent changes, to which these are subject, of proprietors and residences, makes it certain that the great majority of those established in the last ten years are merely substituted for others which existed under other masters and in other places. It displays, however, rather strikingly the amount of private enterprise which positively now prevails; although it does not show to what extent, if any, such enterprise has been more active and productive in recent than in former times. But, with reference to *Public* Day Schools—conducted generally in buildings specially devoted to the purpose of instruction, and not often given up when once begun—the Table seems to testify to the existence of much modern fieal, and proves that within the past ten years a very considerable number of *new* Schools must have been established or that old ones must have been enlarged.

Rate of progress So far, therefore, as our *rate of progress* in school provision and school far from unsatis-attendance is concerned, these facts are far from unsatisfactory; indicating as ia«toiy. they do an immense amount of private and of public energy expended on the field of popular instruction. And this progress is all the more encouraging from the fact that the greater portion of it must have been effected for the *working classes.*

To decide, however, whether the state of things to which the progress thus accomplished has conducted us, while thus comparatively favourable, is satisfactory in itself, we must investigate the other questions: whether the number of children thus at school upon the 31st March 1851 includes the whole or nearly the whole of those who *might* have been there; and whether the instruction they were then receiving was substantial in its nature, and efficiently imparted.

And, first and principally, these inquiries may be put respecting *Day* Schools; since even the warmest friends of the Sunday School do not contend that that most admirable institution is to be considered as a substitute for daily education.

2. *Actual Amount numerically) of Education as compared with the Amount required.*

The population of England and Wales, on the 31st March 1851, being what proportion 17,927,609, the question is, how many of this number ought upon that day to shouhVbong to have been connected with some day school? The question how many ought day schools? to have been then *attending* school will be for after consideration.

To Mr. Edward Baines belongs, in a great degree, the merit of having One out of every brought about a pretty general concurrence of opinion on this point. Before portion accepted the discussions which took place in 1846 upon Jiis estimates, some very Dymost writers, extravagant ideas were afloat upon the subject. This gentleman then estimated, after an apparently careful course of reasoning, that if out of every *nine.* individuals in England one were to be found belonging to some day-school, the proportion would be quite as high as the condition of society in England would permit. Most competent writers are now inclined to assume that one in *eight* would be a satisfactory proportion, after making due allowances for practical impediments. This, on the population of England and Wales (17,927,609), gives 2,240,951 as the number to be under school instruction in 1851. This number, it is said, if constantly connected with day schools, allows an average of *five years and a half* of school instruction to all the children between five and fifteen years of age; and although the fact that the children of the middle and upper classes spend in general *more* than five years at school creates the certainty that the children of the poor spend *less,* yet, even allowing for this reduction, it is argued, the estimate would leave for the children of the labouring classes a period of four or five years' schooling between their fifth and fifteenth years,— a longer time than, practically, children of these classes can be reckoned to remain.f

This calculation, it will be observed, assumes that the 2,240,951 children hh1?mo1Jl0nof (equal to an eighth of the population) enter school not earlier than five and this secure terminate their course not later than fifteen; as, otherwise, there would not be so JfГM" five years long an average of schooling between these ages as above inferred. To see, then, whether in 1851 there was a sufficient number of scholars to fulfil this estimate, we must compare this 2,240,951 with the number of school children *between five and fifteen years of age.* This number (according to a computation from Table H., *post,* page 101.) was 1,768,231 J, or one in rather more than ten; leaving a deficiency of 472,720. On the other hand, if the "one in eight" is to include scholars of all ages, then—although the actual deficiency would only be 96,573 Public Education, by Sir James Kay Shuttleworth, Bart., p. 149.

t Mr. E. Baines's Letters to Lord John Russell. Seventh edition, pp.25—28. t This number is probably very nearly correct, although in the Occupation Tables of the General Census the number returned as "Scholars at School" under Ave was only 227,364. The parents and householders making the Returns, in the latter case, would be not unlikely to leave the column blank in respect of very young children. The idea of considering school study as a ' rank, profession, or occupation." would not naturally occur to the householder; and if the instruction were carefully read, he would see that it restricted the designation to children *upivards of Jive years old.*

B

—the average duration of schooling for each child between five and fifteen would not be five years, but about 4 years; and the length of time which children of the *working classes* could remain at school between their fifth and fifteenth years would be correspondingly reduced—most likely to about *four years.*f Of course, these periods do not comprise the whole time passed at school; since children go there under five years of age; but the period *after* five is so important, that inadequate instruction then would not be compensated by a school attendance at the earlier age.

The varied information gathered at the recent Census, as to the ages and occupations of the people, seems to present facilities for ascertaining by a different process the proportion which might be at school. It may, therefore, be as well to analyse to some extent the general population, so as to see whether, by deducting from the gross number of inhabitants all those who, from certain obvious circumstances, *cannot* be at school, the residue will prove to be an eighth of the entire community, or else so near an eighth as to support the supposition that an eighth would be, as thus computed, a proportion quite as high as could be reasonably looked for to be constantly upon the books of day schools.

1. Those beyond Of course, the first thought which occurs, in looking at the mass of school age. 17,927,609 inhabitants of England and Wales, is, that some are too young and others too old to be at school. Mere infants, therefore, not yet able to receive instruction, and adults who have already passed through their career of education, and are now engaged in active labour, must at once be struck off from this aggregate. But where may immaturity be said to terminate, and where maturity to begin? The age in infancy before attaining which a child is deemed too young for school instruction, and the age in youth upon attaining which a scholar is considered too mature for *furtker* school instruction, vary, of course, according to the different views of different parents. Some send their children to school as early as from three to four, while others retain them at home till five or six. So, some remove their children from school at the age of ten or twelve, whilst others defer this step till the age of sixteen or seventeen. Nevertheless, sufficient agreement exists to enable us to indicate the earliest age at which instruction from home *in general* commences, and the latest age at which it *generally* terminates; and if we fix upon three as the former period, and fifteen as the latter, these perhaps will fairly represent the two extremes beyond which scarcely any day scholars in the ordinary elementary schools can be reasonably expected to be found. Doubtless some few children go to school *before* three, and some stay *later* than fifteen; but as these are *very* few, and as it is no less certain that many remain at home till *after* three, and many (even though without a definite prospect of employment) return from school *before* fifteen, the latter numbers probably would more than balance the former, and leave the period from three to fifteen a tolerably correct representation of the utmost interval appropriated to school instruction in this country. Not that an uninterrupted use of the whole twelve years is thought to be essential to a child's instruction, but that whatever school instruction a child receives (whether for one, for five, for seven or more years,) should be received *within* this interval. All the population, then, beyond these ages (viz., 13,018,913) must be deducted Thus obtained: If we find that out of 2,144,378 scholars, 1,768,231 are between five and fifteen years of age, we may reckon that out of 2,240,951 (t.c. one in eight). 1,847,804 would be between five and fifteen; and this number, when compared with the population between five and fifteen (viz. 4,005,716), produces the above result. t Mr. Baines, of course, was obliged to argue in the absence of statistics as to the number of children under five years of age at school, and he seems to hare under-estimated the proportion.—See " Letters to Lord John Russell:" Letter 4, page 38. mWhat deductions should be made from the general population in order to ascertain the *school population?* from the 17)927,609; the residue will be the number who *are of an age* to be at school, and who ought to be found on the school books, if not prevented by other sufficient causes, such as home education, illness, occupation, &c.

If the preceding *dicta,* as to the limits of school age, be correct, we shall 2. Those em have 4,908,696 children, in England and Wales, who ought to be professedly ployed in la at school, unless prevented by other causes than their age. Of these the Demand For Juvenile Labour is the most important, and will necessitate a further and considerable deduction. Children of the labouring classes are employed at an early age,—some permanently, others temporarily,—at a rate of Jecompence which, though apparently but trifling, is sufficient for their maintenance, and more than sufficient to induce their parents to remove them from school. It is evident that even the lowest amount of wages which the child of a labouring man will receive (from Is. *6d,* to *2s.* per week) must be so great a relief to the parents as to render it almost hopeless that they can withstand the inducement, and retain the child at school in the face of such temptation. And this inducement will be almost equally powerful whether or not the school be one where payments from the children are required. It is not for the sake of *saving a penny* per week that a child is transferred from the school to the factory or the fields, but for the sake of *gaining a shilling or eighteenpence* per week; and the mere opportunity of saving the penny by sending the child to a/ree school would not restrain the parents from making a positive addition to their weekly income if the absence of the child from school could ensure it. Many children obtain permanent employment as early as the age of nine, and all from that age upwards are considered capable of certain kinds of agricultural labour. Indeed some persons qualified to judge are of opinion that the business of a farm labourer cannot be throughly acquired if work be not commenced before eleven or twelve. In mechanical employments labour begins at even an earlier age. Children begin to be employed in factories in needle making, in button making, as errand boys, and in various other capacities, some as early as six, others at any time from 6 to 10. Among the middle classes, children remain longer at school, and the boys become apprentices, &c. at the age of fourteen or fifteen. In very few cases—excepting those where the sons are destined for professional pursuits, are placed by fortune beyond the necessity for labour, or proceed to college—is the period of education protracted beyond 15.

The *extent* to which the demand for juvenile labour interferes with school instruction varies in some degree with the different seasons of the year. In urban occupations and mechanical pursuits, indeed, the demand for labour is not so subject to vicissitude as is the case in agricultural employments. In the latter, children are most wanted in the time of haymaking and harvest, and then there is a temporary decrease in the number of children under school instruction. When these occasional emergencies are satisfied, the extra hands return to school till permanent employment is afforded them. In these cases of merely *temporary* withdrawal from school it is not usual to remove the scholar's name from off the books; no deduction is therefore to be made on this account from the 4,908,696; these occasional absences will not affect the number who ought to be found *professedly* at school *(i.e.* on the books), but only the proportion between this number and the number usually *attending.*

A Table has been prepared representing the number of children, at each quinquennial period under 15, who, at the time of the Census, on the 31st March 1851, were reported as engaged in labour of any kind; and as this was not a season when a sudden want for children's labour would exist, it may be safely assumed that these were *permanently* so engaged, and definitively removed from school. The summary result of this Table is, that of the 4,908,696 children between three and fifteen years of age, 599,829 were occupied in remunerative labour. Of these, 381,774 were males, and 218,055 females.

This Table, however, can hardly be taken as representing *fully* the number of children prevented by labour from attending school; for here the word "occupation" is restricted in its meaning to an *"employment for wages;"* so that many are excluded who, though not receiving wages from a master or mistress, are yet performing all the duties of a servant; the only difference being, that the scene of their labours is their *own home* instead of the house of a stranger. This, of course, applies peculiarly to *girls,* who often at an early age are found so useful, and indeed so indispensable, in household work, that their services are as valuable to their parents as would be the money to be gained by actual servitude. Boys, too, from an early age, are accustomed, in the agricultural districts, to assist their parents in various ways, either in cultivating their allotments or potato grounds, or following them, and waiting upon them in other kinds of labour, in order to become acquainted with the various operations, and acquire a character for aptitude such as may induce the master to employ them.f In towns, a similar assistance can be rendered to the parents in their various trades. In all such cases it appears as if the parents were actuated by a rude conviction that their children were obtaining thus a species of industrial education much more valuable, as bearing on their future temporal lot, than would be the instruction to be gained at school; and, since whatever has relation to the means of livelihood must always exercise the most commanding influence, it cannot be expected that the unmarketable, though great, advantages of mental and moral training should possess in the eyes of parents a value equal to that of those engagements where the child can either actually at once contribute by his service to the maintenance and comfort of the family, or qualify himself for doing so at a very early period.

Neither does the Table include a class, unfortunately too considerable, whose chief or only means of living are the depredations they can make upon society; and yet the frauds and thefts of the criminal population are in many cases as much their ordinary and settled *"occupations"* as the duties of the factory or the farm are the " occupations" of the operative or agricultural labourer. And evidently hopeless is it to expect that any scheme of improved reformatory discipline will avail completely to extinguish an "occupation" which is found to be not only profitable, as supplying means of livelihood, but actually seductive, as accompanied by freedom and excitement.J The utmost effect of even the most judicious plans can only be to *diminish,* not to *abolish,* this predatory class. There will always be a certain number to whom thieving is a daily trade; and the number constantly and wholly thus engaged must be excluded from the estimate of children who should constantly be found at school. I say *wholly* thus engaged, because it is apparent, from the criminal reports, that many juveniles are regular thieves while also filling various situations; therefore it is only such as make thieving their *sole* profession that will have to be deducted upon that account; the others will already have been dealt with in the previous subtraction made on account of children occupied in labour.

Probably it will not be too much to deduct from the numbers between three and fifteen as many as 1,000,000 children, who, from *occupations,* either abroad or at home, cannot be expected to be found at school. This would In agricultural districts, where women are employed in field work, the eldest child remains at home in charge of the younger children. The value of this oversight to the parents is shown by the wages which are commonly paid to a child of the same age when employed in this manner; and this seems to be about *Qd.* per week and food.—Report on the Employment of Women and Children in Agriculture, p. 20.—See also, the Reports of the Government Inspectors of Schools.

t Report on the Employment of Women and Children in Agriculture, pp. 30.119.

t See the evidence of Captain 'Williams and of M M.—Report of Committee on Criminal and Destitute Juveniles. leave 3,908,696 as the number of children of school age who are not prevented by *employment* from attending school.

But a certain number of children will be always *ill*—too ill to be at school. 3. Tho seriously Not merely so indisposed as to be unable to *attends* but so truly ill as to be m" unable even to *belong* to any school, or to appear upon its books. A number equal to *five per cent,* of the number last obtained (3,908,696), or 195,435, would be, perhaps, a fair deduction upon this account, diminishing the number to be always found upon the school books to 3,713,261.

But a certain amount of education is obtained *at home*. The number of Those educhildren returned by the householders as thus instructed, at the Census, was 44,625; of whom 17,302 were males, and 27,323 females. These were all apparently receiving instruction from tutors or governesses not members of the family. The direction on the "Householder's Schedule" with reference to the occupations of children was to the effect that, in the case of children under education at home, they should be returned as "Scholars at home," *if above five years of age,* and if receiving daily regular instruction under a Tutor or Governess. The instruction was not implicity obeyed, as some children though under five years of age were returned as "Scholars at home;" but some allowance ought perhaps to be made for children under five, who were actually receiving regular tuition at home though not returned so. To raise the total number of scholars at home, between three and fifteen years of age, to 50,000 (19,386 males and 30,614 females) would probably meet the case. No doubt, a further number of the *younger* children were under the tuition of the elder. If, however, we decline to recognise the latter, probably irregular, instruction, as an adequate substitute for systematic training by professional teachers, and deduct but the 50,000; the residue of children between three and fifteen, having no impediment of age, occupation, serious sickness, or domestic education, to detain them from school, would be 3,663,261.

It does not occur to me that any further deductions should be made in order Number of chilto obtain a strict estimate of the number of children *capable* of being at school; jjjljjw?t *e* a *strict* estimate being understood to refer to the number simply who have health and leisure to attend. No deduction, therefore, is made on account of pauper children, since their education is, or ought to be, (by general consent,) provided by the state; nor on account of youthful prisoners, since their instruction also is, or ought to be, provided in like manner; nor for the children of the very poor, unable or unwilling to defray the school expense, since no one now contends that the parents' poverty is any valid reason why the children should remain in ignorance,—the only question being, by what agency should their instruction be secured. The 3,663,261 therefore which remain after the deductions caused by age, employment, illness, and home educaction, will be the maximum number which could be at school, in the most auspicious circumstances—parents being universally convinced of the advantages of education to their offspring, and possessing the ability (either from their own resources or with the aid of others) to procure it for them.

But, doubtless, our attainment to a state of things so satisfactory as this is Ac,ertn.lati ., tudeol discretion beyond the reach of hope. The continued presence at school or every child must be allowed between three and fifteen years of age, while having health and leisure, would to Parent!, presume in the parents an amount of intelligent appreciation of instruction such as probably the utmost improvement in the mode and matter of education, even if accompanied by utmost cheapness, never will produce. To realize all this would be to realize Utopia; for, practically, of course, the duration cf children's schooling is regulated not by the possible amount of time which *might* be thus appropriated, but by the parents' views of what is a *sufficient* period. And as, in England, neither the opinions nor the acts of parents, with respect to this, are likely to be influenced by aught but moral means, it seems quite clear that we must be content, for some time yet, with a position lower considerably than this. Perhaps not one in ten of English parents keeps a child at school for twelve years constantly, from three to fifteen years of age; some, doubtless, thinking that to keep a child at home till five does not prevent its future acquisition of as much instruction as will ever be of use, and others thinking that by twelve or thirteen quite an adequate amount of useful knowledge has already been acquired. There will thus be always a considerable number of children neither at school, nor ill, nor yet employed; and if, regarding only what is practicable, we forego the absolute and arbitrary standard previously reached, and accept as a legitimate cause of absence, the discretion, within reasonable limits, of the parents, it is evident that another and not small deduction must be made from the number of children between three and fifteen years of age before we can obtain an estimate of the number which, in a well-instructed nation, should be constantly connected with some dayschool.

What, then, is the probable extent of the deduction to be made on this account? Of course, I do not here pretend to offer more than a suggestion, to be dealt with by the many competent authorities to whom the subject is much more familiar than to me. And the number which I venture to suggest must not be taken as the number which, in the present moral condition of the people, can be reasonably *expected* to be found in day schools; but the number which *should* be there, and which may be adopted as a standard up to which we ought to work. Assuming, then, that the school instruction of a child ought not at all events to be procrastinated until after *five,* and that, health and leisure being both possessed, it ought not to be relinquished earlier than *twelve*,—in other words, assuming that parental duty might be properly discharged although the child might not be sent to school till five years old, and although it might not be retained there after reaching twelve,—the further deduction to be made from the 3,663,261 would be— all the children between three and five not under professional education, nor ill (vifi. 574,611), and all the children between twelve and fifteen neither at school, nor professionally instructed at home, nor ill, nor in employment (vifi. 73,245f). The residue would be 3,015,405; consisting, in the first place, of all between five and twelve not occupied, nor receiving professional home instruction, nor kept from school by illness—and, in the second place, of all such below five or above twelve as their parents choose to send to school, or to retain there.

Besidue, after This residue appears to me to fairly represent the number of children, all deductions. between tnree and fifteen, which in a population of 17,927,609 should be found upon the books of all the various day schools, in order to ensure an adequate amount of education, at a proper school age, for the whole of the English people. The proportion is one in *six* of the total population; and as the aggregate population increases, the number of scholars should increase by as many as is requisite to keep up a continual supply equivalent to one in *six*—provided that the proportion between five and twelve be never less than That is — 902,980 less 278,617 educated at school and 4,C03 under paid instructors at home, and 43,19111 (who have been before deducted—being included in the 195,435). It is here assumed that the proportion of children under five ill is the same as above Ave; though probably the percentage of illness is somewhat higher at the earlier years. The number 4,603 is that which is given in the Occupation Tables as the number educated at home *under Jive*: it is assumed they were all between three and five.

t On the preceding supposition that 1,000,000 children altogether are employed, either for their parents or for others, the proportion between 12 and 15, according to Table 2, would be 748,067. The number at school between 12 and 15, according to Table 2. is 285,151; and the number receiving paid instruction at home would be 8,031. The number ill would amount to 19,286 The whole number of children between 12 and 15 being 1,133,780, the residue would be as above, 73,245. ninety-four per cent. of those unoceupied between these ages (the remaining six per cent. being allowed for sickness and home education). The legal period in Prussia is from five to fourteen: the concessions made by the preceding estimate on account of the different industrial organifiation of the English people are—to allow the elementary education to finish (if the parents choose)

at twelve in lieu of fourteen, and to take as a sufficient reason for school absence the simple fact of a child's *employment,* however premature the age at which his, occupation is commenced. Doubtless, such premature employment is incompatible with adequate instruction; but, without compulsory regulations, the adoption of which appears to be approved by no one, little hope can be indulged that this impediment to school attendance will be even gradually removed. But if a child is *not* at work, his absence from school at any time between five and twelve can only be occasioned either by the parents' inability » to sustain the school expense, or else by their unreasonable disesteem of education—neither of which causes can at all avail to lower the preceding estimate.

If this can be accepted as a practicable standard, we at once perceive that Ourpreaent we at present fall considerably short of it. The following Table (1.) will exhibit, this standard. in some degree, the extent to which children between 5 and 12, who are unemployed in remunerative occupations, are nevertheless withheld from school. It is taken from the householders' returns, and represents the way in which the column headed "Rank, Profession, or Occupation" was filled up with reference to 253,425 children between three and fifteen years of age.f It will therefore include children educated at home.

Table 1.

Present average If the proportions in the previous Table (1.) be applied to the actual number duration of ,,...., i ,, . ',. rr schooling. or children *in the whole of hngland and Wales,* in connexion with the ascer tained facts about their ages in quinquennial periods and their occupations, we shall get the following view:—

So that, while the total number of day scholars (at school) in England and Wales at all ages is 2,144,378, out of a population of 17,927,609, being in the proportion of one to 8-£, the number of day scholars between three and fifteen years of age is 2,046,848 out of a population, between those years, of 4,908,696, being in the proportion of one to 2f-; and the number between five and fifteen is 1,768,231 out of a population of 4,005,716, being in the proportion of one to 2f. The average schooltime, therefore, of all the children in England and Wales between their third and fifteenth years is as nearly as possible 5 years, and between their fifth and fifteenth years it is 4-f years.

But as some (the children of the middle and upper classes) doubtless spend *more* than five years at school between three and fifteen, and more than 4f years between five and fifteen, the average for the children of the working classes must be *less* than 5 years and 4f years respectively—probably not more than 4-years in the former case and 4 years in the latter. That is— assuming that all the children of working parents are under education—every child would spend at school but four years out of the twelve which elapse between five and fifteen.f Taking all the children together, without distinction *Beaminster, Bcthnal Green, Hinckley, Walsingham, Westbury, Williton, Mildenhall, York,*

Settle, Shoreditch, Evesham, Gainsborough, Longtoum, Chapel-en-le-Frith, Sedbergh, Pateleu

Bridge, Rothbury, Ledbury, Birmingham, Holbcach, Bromsgrove, Bourn, Llanrwst, Blandford,

Liverpool, Lceds. The total population of these localities, at all ages, is Males 496,467, Females 514,710.

Tho number of scholars at school (2,144,378) is taken from the *Educational* Returns in preference to the Occupation Tables.

t The average length of schooling for children of all classes, between these periods is as nearly as possible 4f years. I assume the children of tho middle and upper classes to be about *& fourth* of class, the average amount of schooling received within certain intervals (supposing all to receive education) appears to be as follows:

The age at which a child becomes fitted to enter upon a course of primary Not sufficient school instruction is generally stated to be upon the completion of the yancedages *sixth* year. The schools for children who have not attained that age are mostly infant schools, in character if not by name. It seems to be admitted pretty generally amongst educationists that unless a good proportion o e schooling which a child receives be given above the age of six, its value is considerably diminished, and cannot be looked upon as adequate. Upon this theory the facts above produced appear to indicate a state of education far from satisfactory; since the average length of schooling received by children of *all 'classes* between six and fifteen cannot exceed four years, and the average for children of the working classes cannot much exceed three years. So that, while upon an average the children of the labouring classes may perhaps (if all are under education) have 4 years of schooling, a very considerable part of their instruction is imparted during what may be described as the "infant period." or other.

The actual number of separate scholars during the above-named periods Number receivcannot be with certainty inferred from these statistics. They by no means prove for soTM period that all the children in England obtain 5 years' schooling in the interval between their third and fifteenth years, but merely that it is consistent with these figures that they all *might* do so—some being instructed at one part of the twelve years, and some at another part. Upon the other hand, it is equally consistent with these figures that some might be instructed for a longer period than 5 years out of the twelve, others being instructed for a shorter; or, again, that some might be at school for the whole twelve years, and others not get any instruction at all. Without assistance from extraneous sources we can only know that, supposing our educational position to continue as-in 1851, and the population to be also stationary, we should, on visiting twelve years after all the schools of England, still find 2,046,848 children, between three and fifteen years of age, receiving education. This fact would prove that an amount of school-time equal to 24,562,176 years had been consumed between 1851 and 1863; but amongst how many individual children this amount of school-time had been shared would not be known, nor yet the sifie (if I may so express it) of particular shares. For aught which the figures would reveal, the whole of the children in England might have been at school for five years each; or half the children might have been at school for eight years each, and the other half for two years each; or a third of the children might have been at of the whole, and that they attend school six years out of the ten. If they form more than a fourth of the juvenile population, or if they attend more than six years, the average length of

Equally unsatisfactory whether a limited number be instructed for an adequate period, or a great number for a limited period.

Attendance at school.

school for ten years each, another third for five years each, and the remaining third not at all. The mere number always to be found upon the school books does not indicate, without the aid of another element, the number which receives instruction more or less. The other element required to solve this problem is, the average period during which the 2,046,848 scholars actually ascertained to be at school remain there; and if we have recourse to the opinions and experience of able writers and instructors on this point, the inference seems to be, that, while among the middle and upper classes the average time expended on their children's school-education is about six years, the average time amongst the labouring classes cannot much exceed four years. If this be so, the inference appears inevitable, that very few children are *completely* uninstructed; nearly all, at some time or another of their childhood, see the inside of a schoolroom, although some do little more. Upon no other supposition can the constant presence on the school books of the names of upwards of 2,000,000 children between three and fifteen out of 4,908,696 be consistent with a brief school period for any considerable portion of the former number. Probably it is not easy to determine which is the more unsatisfactory,—an absence of instruction altogether for a certain portion of the population while the rest are tolerably educated, or a meagre and resultless education given to the whole. The unpleasant choice of evils lies between a wide extent of inefficient schooling and a limited extent of more effective teaching, contemporary with a certain portion, also limited, of utter ignorance. 'Whichever of these two alternatives be taken as deseribing our existing state, there ought to be a larger number than 2,046,848 children between three and fifteen years of age at the various day schools, if an adequate extent of education is to be afforded; in the latter case, in order that the whole community might be instructed—in the former case, in order that the whole, assumed to be already under education, might remain so for a longer period. Unless as many as 3,000,000 children out of 4,908,696 between those ages can be always found upon the books of day schools, we cannot be sure that some considerable number may not be entirely uninstructed, or that those among the poorer classes who *do* go to school remain there long enough to learn.f

The need, too, thus assumed, of a constant supply upon the school books of 3,000,000 children between three and fifteen (or three fifths of the number between those ages) will be more apparent if it be remembered that the fact of *belonging* to a day school does not imply continuous *attendance*. It is found, that in private schools the number of children attending on any particular day is 91 per cent. of the number belonging to such schools; while in "The master of every National School finds he must lay in his account for making the best of a year or fimeen months in great cities, and for two years and a half in less populous places." " We have only possession of the minds of the children sent to our National Schools for one or two years, or at most three."—Rev. R. Burgess, Letter to Sir James Graham, 1842.

"I have taken some pains to ascertain one very important fact, as especially bearing upon religious instruction; I mean the average time for children remaining in our best schools when we get them there; and X believe it will be found that the average does not extend, in large towns and manufacturing districts, to more than fifteen months for boys, and somewhat less for girls. In some of our seaports I find it extend to two years and a half, and occasionally three years; but I have very little hesitation in allirming that throughout England the average time passed by the children of our poor and industrious classes does not exceed two years: and, if we confine ourselves to the populous places, eighteen months will be an ample allowance under the most favourable circumstances."—Rev. R. Burgess, Letter to Dr. Hook, 1847.

"The average duration seems to lie less than two years — one year and three quarters is probably the time — in which the chief instruction of their whole life is to he given. I speak here of the time spent in the juvenile school, and not in the infants'."—Rlav. I. Watkins's Report, Minutes of Council, 1845, vol. H. p. 178.

t Supposing that the children of the middle and upper classes form *& fourth* part of the whole number of children between three and fimeen (i.e. a fourth of 4,908,696), and that they may in future belong to day schools for eight years, on an average, out of the twelve; then, upon the assumption that 8,000,000 scholars between those ages (or one in six of the total population) are always to be found on the books of day schools, the 3,681,522 children of the labouring classes would belong to day schools for seven years, on an average; a length of time which is incom' natible with less than an almost universal educationcontiuuing too for an adequate peripd beyond the *infant* school age. *public* schools the number in attendance is 79 per cent. of the number on the books. So that while, as shown before, the average period during which a child remains at school between three and fifteen (on the supposition that all go to school) is close upon five years, the average time which each child passes in the actual receipt of education is not more than *4* years (including holidays). If out of 4,908,696 children between three and fifteen there could be 3,000,000 found upon the books of day schools (equal to about one in six of the total population, or three fifths of the number between those ages,) there would then be some security, not only that as many as possible of the inhabitants of England were belonging for an adequate period to some day school, but also that they were for an adequate period in actual receipt of education.

How far *evening schools* for children can be looked upon as substitutes for Evening schools day schools, or as lengthening the period of school-time, is a question very Howte«?subdiflicult to answer, in the absence of a general systematic method of conducting stitute for day such establishments. Unfortunately no inquiry as to these was instituted at the Census; so that the determination of this question must be mainly left to those whose information on the subject qualifies them to decide; but since, if the preceding calculations have been free from any grievous error, no insuperable impediments prevent the constant presence on the books of *day* schools of three fifths of the children between three and fifteen years of age—

the greatest hindrance, the insensibility of parents, being one which we may hope will, either by the natural progress of society, or, yet more likely, by the progress of religion, be in time removed—it may perhaps be not unreasonable to take that proportion as the standard with which to compare our actual position. The result of such comparison, applied to the figures of 1851, appears to be, that an addition of about 970,000 scholars between the ages of five and twelve would have raised us up to that desirable standard—assuming that the 2,144,378 already under education were in schools *efficiently conducted.*

This is the next subject of inquiry.

3. *Quality of existing instruction in Day Schools.*

The materials which the Census furnishes for estimating the character of the instruction given to the 2,144,378 scholars found belonging to the various day schools in March 1851, are principally these:—the subjects which the children were professedly engaged in learning, and the number of children learning each— the various amounts which children pay for their instruction—the remuneration which the teachers gain for their exertions—and some other and more incidental indications. None of these materials, perhaps, in the form in which alone they are presentable, supply conclusive information; but enough will probably be found from which to draw some general inference.

In the 44,836 school establishments of England and Wales from which Number of returns were received, it appears that boys were taught (alone or along with instructionis girls) in 41,035 (14,995 public and 26,040 private), while girls were taught uiar branct (alone or along with boys) in 40,016 (14,084 public and 25,932 private). If of learning. we consider, for the sake of the comparison, each of these as a separate school, it will appear that out of 33,993 boys' schools, concerning which information was given (12,741 public and 21,252 private), there were 33,315 in which *reading* was being taught,

23,288 in which *writing* was being taught, 13,532 in which *geography* was being taught, &c.; while out of 32,928 girls' schools (11,837 public and 21,091 private), there were 32,396 in which *reading* was being taught, 24,402 in which *writing* was being taught, 13,770 in which *geography* was being taught, &c. The number in which instruction was given in each of the eleven

Materials furnished by the Census for conclusions on this point.

Number of A similar view with respect to *scholars* can be given for 1,818,024 children structed in par-out of the 2,144,378, viz. for 1,240,093 connected with public schools (699,167 tfteEnt£nChS8 males and 640926 females), and for 577,931 connected with private schools (289,448 males and 288,483 females). The result is given in Table 4.

To find in the schools a large proportion of the children learning the mere Too large a prorudiments of knowledge, while a small proportion only is engaged upon the merefy rudihigher branches, must be looked upon as an unfavourable sign; revealing mentaryinstrucprobably. a limited duration of instruction—received, too, at an early age. And when it is remembered that, of those who appear to have been engaged in the more advanced departments of instruction, a majority were probably belonging to the upper and the middle classes, a preceding speculation seems to be corroborated, that the children of the working classes go to school while very young, and remain but for a very scanty period. On this account perhaps it would be hasty to assume that the mass of teachers in these schools was composed of persons having limited acquirements; since, of course, the character of the instruction given must depend upon the scholars' capacity to receive, and, if children uniformly leave school at an early age, it is impossible that they should ever advance beyond mere elementary instruction.

A rough attempt to classify according to efficiency the 29,425 private schools Classification of which sent Returns produced the following result:— according to 8 1. Superior. (Classical, Boarding, Proprietary, Ladies', &c.)- 4,956 efficiency.
2. Middling. (Commercial, &c.'; teaching arithmetic, English grammar, and geography)---7,095 3. Inferior. (Principally *dame* schools; only reading and writing taught, the latter not always)... 13,879 Undescribed...-.--3,495 29,425
The distinction is, of course, in some measure arbitrary—the returns not always furnishing the means for an unhesitating judgment; but I believe it does not represent unfairly the actual state of things with reference to private schools. Of course, in looking at the 13,879 inferior schools, it must not be forgotten what a large proportion of the total number of scholars was composed of children *under five years old,* for whom a higher class of school would be of little avail. But it will probably be felt that, after all allowances on this account, the number given above, if accurate, is too considerable.—In the case of 708 out of these 13,879, the returns were respectively signed by the master or mistress with a *mark.* The same is noticeable with respect to 35 *Public Schools,* most of which had small Endowments.

The efficiency of a school depends, unquestionably, more upon the efficiency JjjJJjJ of the *teacher* than upon any other circumstance. The information given in the Census Returns, by which we may approximate towards a definite conception of the present state of the teachers in our public schools, is of two kinds; first, we are informed of the respective numbers of adult and juvenile instructors—distinguishing how many of the latter are stipendiary and how many are gratuitous; and secondly, we are informed at what rate, on the average, stipendiary teachers (both adult and juvenile) are recompensed. The mere *number* of teachers in 11,420 public schools, from which out of 15,411 information on the point was given (containing 1,142,892 scholars), is as follows:—

The efficiency of these instructors may, no doubt, in some degree be measured by the average amount of their remuneration; for although a certain number of very competent teachers may perhaps be found receiving very scanty incomes, yet in general the ill-paid teacher will be either ill-adapted for his post or else neglectful of its duties. Table N. in the Summary Tables *(post, page 108)* exhibits, with respect to *Lancashire* and *Lincolnshire,* the average emoluments of 1,002 instructors. The investigation has been necessarily, from want of time, restricted to these counties; which perhaps may be regarded as fair indications of the state of things elsewhere.

Modern improvements in the training of Teachers.

It has long been obvious, to those who have at heart the improved instruction of the people, that the most essential step towards the attainment of that end is the improved condition of the teacher. Both the "British" and the "National" Societies, from the earliest period of their career, devoted much attention to the training of efficient teachers for the schools connected with them. In 1818, the former sent out forty-five teachers; in 1828, nearly double, viz., eighty-seven; in 1838, as many as 183; and in 1852, but little less, viz., 163. The latter society as early as 1811, commenced a training institution, and it now has five such colleges connected specially with itself, which send out yearly about 270 teachers. Since the formation of the Committee of Council on Education these colleges have greatly increased in number. At present there are about 40 in England and Wales, sustained at an annual cost of about 90,000/. Of these, 34 are connected with the Church of England, one belongs to the British and Foreign School Society, one to the Roman Catholics, one to the Wesleyan Methodists, one to the Congregationalists, and one to the Voluntary School Association. All of these, except the two last mentioned, receive assistance from the parliamentary grants. The sum expended from this source towards the *building* of these institutions has been about 120,000/. out of a total cost of about 310,000/. f The training institution of the Congregationalists cost 12,000/., contributed entirely from their own resources. The number of students who could be accommodated in these colleges is about 2,000; the cost of their education being computed at *50l.* per annum each for males, and 40/. per annum for females. By the operation of the Minutes of Council of 1846 the Government sustains a share of the expense in reference to two descriptions of such students, viz.: (1.), a certain number of young persons of superior merit, who on that account are selected from the elementary schools to proceed to the training colleges—being called " Queen's Scholars;" and (2.), such other persons as, entering on their own account, receive certificates of merit from the Government inspectors. For each "0.ueen's Scholar" the Government pays to the To Sir James Kay Shuttleworth, Bart., belongs the great merit, if not of creating, of having given an extraordinary impulse to the modern movement for providing Training Colleges. In conjunction with Mr. Tufliiell he, in 1840, established an experimental training college at Battersca, which soon gave practical evidence of the immense advantage of the plan.

t I'ublic Education. By Sir Jamea Kay Shuttleworth, Bait., p. 66. training college *20l.* for the first year, 25/. for the second, and 30/. for the third, and an additional *20l.* at the end of the first year if the progress of the student has been satisfactory. For each of the other students Government pays varying sums between *20l.* and *30l.*

The tendency of these measures is to secure that the training colleges, so far as they are under government inspection, shall receive, direct from the elementary schools, a constant stream of students, who have given promise of ability, and shown an aptitude for teaching. Thus is being much accelerated the revolution which was gradually taking place in the monitorial system. This had already been perceived to be, in its original shape, as introduced by Bell and Lancaster, inadequate to the occasion; and the size of individual schools had constantly been lessening, till from 1,000 scholars to one master, as was formerly conceived to be a practicable number—and indeed a striking indication of success—a maximum of somewhere about 200 had been fixed as the limit of efficient supervision. It was seen that the continual changes in the ranks of monitors, occasioned by their necessary transference from the school to the field or the factory, much detracted from the value of their youthful aid, and made it necessary to increase the proportion of purely professional instructors. This the plans of Government were calculated to secure, while yet retaining all the best results of juvenile assistance. By offering gratuities of from 10/. to 20/. a year to such of the most eligible monitors as would consent to be apprenticed for five years to some competent master or mistress, and from *5l.* to *2l.* 10s. to such as, without apprenticeship, would continue in the school till the age of seventeen,—by these means, it was thought, in combination with the plan already mentioned of Queen's scholarships in training colleges, the monitorial system would be rendered vastly more effective and a source prepared from which an adequate supply of able future teachers might be drawn. The elementary school was thus designed to be a nursery to the training college, and inducements were held forth to skilful monitors to look to teaching as the occupation of their lives. f It appears that in August 1853, the number of pupil-teachers who had completed their term of apprenticeship was 1371, of whom 942 were males and 429 females.

And while thus, under the' Minutes of Council, plans have been devised for securing youthful talent for the work of education, and for training it effectively when thus secured, the augmentation of the stipends of adult instructors has not been omitted from the schemes of the same Department. Independently of grants of from *3l.* to *5l.* for each apprentice, and of *l.* 10s. to *2l.* 10s. for every stipendiary monitor (in return for which the master or mistress is to give them instruction for an hour and a half a day for five days in the week), annual sums of from *5l.* to *30l.* are given to such as have passed one or more years in an inspected training college and received an annual inspector's certificate of merit, on condition that the school-trustees provide a house rent-free, and a further salary at least double the amount of grant.

The number of teachers who had apprentices in 1851 appears to have been 1,173, and the number of such apprentices (or pupil teachers) 5,607.

Considerable improvements in the *method* of teaching, and in the character of the school books and school apparatus, &c, have also been, of late years, introduced in most of the schools which are subject to Government inspection, In Germany and Switzerland the number of children to a teacher rarely exceeds 80, and is often not above 50. In large schools there are several class rooms in which classes of children are taught — each class by a separate teacher.—" The Condition and Education of Poor Children in English and German Towns." By Joseph Kay. 1853. t Another inducement was also held out by the Minutes of 184fl, viz. that such pupil teachers as might not display the highest qualifications for the office of schoolmaster, but whose conduct and attainments were satisfactory, should have opened to them an opportunity of obtaining employment in the public service. This, however, was withdrawn some five years afterwards 1 as it probably appeared that those who were least qualified for schoolmasters would scarcely be the and in many others. The nature and extent of these important alterations may be seen by reference to the published Minutes of Council on Education, and to the reports of the principal educational societies.

The conclusion, however, can be scarcely avoided that, whatever may be the prospect before us of attaining, at no distant period hence, a great accession to the number of efficiently conducted day schools, the actual *present* state of many must be far from satisfactory.

Besult of the The result of this attempt to answer the three questions upon which depends quiries. the answer to the other question, whether our present educational position as siiouWbeupou" t ay schools is satisfactory or not? appears to be as follows: The number of the school children in England and Wales of an age appropriate to school instruction (say from three to fifteen) is 4,908,696; from which must be deducted, as unable on account of occupation, serious illness, or domestic education, to belong to day schools, 1,245,435; leaving a residue of 3,663,261 with respect to whom there is apparently no reason other than the parents' pleasure why they should not be at school. Allowing the parents' discretion to be reasonable, while the child is under the age of five and after it has passed the age of twelve, there yet remain as many as 968,557 children between five and twelve whose absence from the schoolbooks cannot be explained by either illness, occupation, professional home instruction, or legitimate excuse of parents. Further; it appears that some of the existing schools are inefficient—ill adapted for their purpose; so that, to have made, the state of things in 1851 completely satisfactory, there should have been 968,557 more scholars between the ages of five and twelve upon the school-books, while some of those already there should have been found at more efficient schools.

This would establish a proportion of 16-8 per cent. of the total population; 1'5 per cent. between three and five— 1"6 per cent. between twelve and fifteen— and 13-7 per cent. between five and twelve. There seems no valid reason why that proportion should not be continually upon the books of day schools: none with respect to the 1 5 per cent. between three and five, because that number is already found there; none with respect to the 16 per cent. between twelve and In connexion with the question of the quality of existing education, the test of *wantage marks* can scarcely be passed over. This test, though not in all respects infallible — as the art of writing is with great facility forgotten by tho poor, who find no useful application for it, while from various causes some who *can* write nevertheless decline to sign the register —is certainly of some considerable value, as exhibiting from year to year what *progress* is effected. If from time to time an *increase* or a *diminution* in the number of marks, proportioned to the number of marriages. is manifested, then, although no positive criterion perhaps can be presumed, the inference is almost unavoidable, that education at the periods respectively at which one portion of the married persons was at school must have been either more or less effective than it was when the other portion was at school. If at the end of a ten years' interval tho number of marks is less in proportion to the marriages than it was at the beginning of tho interval, this seems to.show that (the average age of marriage being 25) the state of education 15 years before the more recent date was better than it was 10 years earlier, or else that more inducements to retain the knowledge once acquired were existing at the former period than at the latter. It appears, from the Registrar General's Eleventh Annual Report, that the number of marks per cent. in 1839 was 41'8, in 1840 it was 42'0, and in 1841 it was 40'8; while in 1851 tho proportion had declined to 38'0. So that, judging from this test, instruction was more effective, or the art of writing was better retained, in the period 1833-38 than it was 10 years before (1823-28). The improvement seems to have been nearly equal in each sex; the proportion of marks by males having fallen from 33"7 per cent. in 1839 to 30'8 per cent. in 1851; while the proportion of marks by females fell from 49-5 in 1839 to 45'3 per cent. in 1851. The average age of marriage being 25, the marks appearing in the registers of 1851 must be attributed to the neglect of 15 or 18 years ago when the persons married were in their school-age: the extent and value of the education given in more recent years (so far as the same can be inferred from marriage-marks) can only bo exhibited by taking the marriages of *younger* persons; and if the marriages of *minors* in 1851 be taken (which will probably show what was being taught, and how, about 10 years ago), the extraordinary fact presents itself that of 31,987 minors married in 1851 (7,737 males and 24,250 females), no less than 52'6 per cent. were unable to sign their names (vifi. 42 7 per cent. of the males and 55'8 per cent. of the females). This, however, can hardly betaken as a criterion of the whole community of minors, or even of the whole of the minors of tho labouring class; since, doubtless, those who married early and improvidently were not favourable specimens of minors who refrained from marriage. Still, they must represent a too considerable number, and the aspect of things from this view is discouraging.

fifteen, because *that* number also is already there; and none with respect to the 13'7 per cent. between five and twelve, because, not being occupied in labour either at home or away from home, their absence from school cannot be serviceable to their parents. With respect to these 3,000,000 children, out of 18,000,000 persons there appears no obstacle of immaturity, of illness, of employment, of professional home education, to prevent their connection with some day school. These, at all events, should be invariably found upon the school-books, since no tangible inducement stronger than the saving of a few pence weekly operates to make the parents keep their children from the school; and this inducement, nearly all admit, should be removed—if necessary, by the aid of others, whether furnished as a voluntary charity or by the State. Any further number could be added only as the parents should so learn the worth of education as to yield for it the positive sacrifice of their children's *earnings*.

Supposing, then, that 168 per cent. (or one in six) of the population might (so far as any *valid* hindrance is concerned) have been upon the school-books in 1851, two questions occur with reference to the sources from which this proportion should have been supplied. First, should each of the *sexes* contribute 16-8 per cent. of the total population of that sex? and secondly, should each *locality* contribute 16' 8 per cent. of the population of that locality.

As to the *sexes,* they were far from furnishing, in 1851, an equal number of

JjJJ scholars; for while, out of 8,781,225 males there were 1,157,685 scholars (or proportions of 13-2 per cent.), out of 9,146,384 females there were only 986,693 scholars (or Boholarsf 10-8 per cent.). If we include the scholars *at home,* the proportion will be slightly more favourable for the females, the male scholars being 1,177,071 against 1,017,307 female scholars (or 13'4 per cent. against ll"lper cent.). This actual difference shows, no doubt, that girls are taken away from school in very great numbers at a very early age to attend to various household avocations. But, considering how vast an influence is exercised by female character upon the general disposition of society, it cannot but appear of very great importance that the future wives and mothers of the people should be qualified by sound and healthy education, continued for the longest practicable period, to exert a softening and an elevating influence upon their partners and their offspring. So that, if the proportion of 16 8 per cent. between three and fifteen be taken as the standard, and if each of the sexes ought to have contributed in 1851 that proportion of its number to the day schools, there should have been about 370,000 more male scholars, and about 600,000 more female scholars.

As to *locality,* it will be found impossible to secure an equal proportion of o"ᵀᴍ?. scholars to the total population in places which so vary in their social circum-an equal prostances as do many of the English town and country parishes. Where manu-Molars?' facturing industry is active, there a great demand will constantly exist for youthful labour; there more children in proportion to the total population will be found than in other places; and a greater portion of the whole population will belong to the working classes. These peculiarities will necessarily produce a shortening of the period which children upon an average can be expected to pass at school. As great a proportion of children might go to school in a manufacturing town as in a rural parish of the same population, and yet there might not be so many constantly at school in the former as in the latter,—the reason being that the children in the town would stay at school for a *shorter period* than would the children in the country, who, in consequence of a much less demand for early labour, would possess more leisure for prolonged instruction. Therefore, in considering the state and estimating the requirements of c particular localities, each place must be discussed, in great degree, with reference to its own peculiar industrial condition; and it must not be expected that in Manchester or Bradford, Birmingham or Wolverhampton, such a large proportion of the total population should be found in day schools as in other places where the wheels of industry are not so restless, and its claims upon the young are less inexorable. Probably, in such localities the people seek in other ways the education which they cannot spare the time to get in day schools; and the number and the character of *Evening* schools and *Sunday* schools, and the average attendance at them, must be looked at, ere a true opinion can be formed upon the educational position of such places, as compared with that of others. The reasonable proportion, if the previous estimate can be admitted, would be just what would be yielded by taking all the children between five and twelve *not otherwise employed,* nor ill, nor educated at home, and adding to this the numbers under five and above twelve *actually at school.* There would thus be an *aggregate* proportion for the whole of England and Wales of 16'8 per cent.; but the proportion would not be uniform throughout the country—varying according to the various conditions of particular localities. But no safe comparison can be attempted between different localities, unless the size of each be so considerable as to obviate the risk of fallacy, arising from the fact that in many cases schools in one locality are partly filled by children belonging to another. Subject to these qualifications, the following statement will show how far each of the English counties falls below the standard which has been suggested as desirable, and not, with some exertion, unattainable:—

Assuming, then, that 3,000,000 scholars might (as far as mere ability and opportunity are concerned) have been found upon the school-books in 1851, the great and practical question, as afFecting future effort, is, why were they *not* there? What were the causes which prevented 968,557 healthy unemployed children between the ages of five and twelve from being then in receipt of daily education? If we can determine what are the most prevalent impediments to school attendance, we shall probably obtain from hence the clearest indications of the most appropriate remedies.

What are the causes of the deficiency of scholars f 1. The want of *school accommodation* is perhaps the very least of these 1-Deficiency impediments. From apprehension that inquiries on this point would not be *modationf0* answered so as to admit of any. sound, statistical result, no questions were inserted in the Census schedule as to the capacity of schools with reference to the number of scholars that could be instructed in them; but it is not difficult to gain, from other sources, a tolerably accurate idea of the proportion which in general obtains between the number of scholars in attendance and the total number which could be accommodated. Mr. Watkins, one of the Government inspectors, reports that in 256 inspected schools, having 27,363 children in average attendance, the accommodation, at six square feet for each child, was available for 50,801; while at eight square feet for each child (which appears to be considered the more reasonable allowance) the accommodation was for 38,101. In Manchester and Salford, it seems from the evidence before the Parliamentary Committee of 1852, while only 33,663 children were upon the books of all the day schools, there was *redundant* accommodation for no less than 34,443. So that it may very fairly be concluded, that if, in 1851, as many as 2,144,378 scholars were upon the books of day schools, the *accommodation* could not have been far from adequate for 3,000,000. It is possible, indeed, that the accommodation may not have been always just in the place where it was wanted; and of course, if out of the reach of those requiring education, it was practically worthless; but there seems no room for doubt that in a multitude of cases where great numbers of children live from day to day without instruction, they have actually in the very midst of them an ample school provision,—many buildings being occupied by barely half the number of scholars who might daily assemble in them. In the face of such neglect of present opportunities of education, it can scarcely be maintained, perhaps, that an inadequate amount of *room* is a potent reason why so many children are continually absent from school.

2. The *poverty* of many parents, and their consequent inability to pay the 2. Poverty of usual school fee, has been alleged as another and an influential cause of the tlle parentschildren's absence; and, unquestionably, poverty in many cases does so seriously press upon the labouring man, that the education of his children, even at the seemingly trifling cost of 1d. or *2d.* weekly, is impossible; but the plea is scarcely satisfactory to any great extent beyond the purely *pauper* class; and indoor pauper children are already educated by the State. For when it is considered that the working classes annually spend upon intoxicating liquors nearly 50,000,000/. sterling,f it can hardly be asserted generally that the children are retained at home because the parents are unable to advance *d.* or *2d.* per week. Unquestionably, if by "poverty" is meant the incompatibility of the child's instruction with some personal indulgence of the parents, this points out the real cause why, both among the working classes and also among the other classes, many children are detained at home who ought to be at school; but this reveals much less a physical than a moral obstacle—a hindrance less resulting from the want of means than from the want of inclination; in short, a low appreciation by the parents of the value of instruction to their children, in comparison with those more sensual enjoyments to themselves for the sake of which it is neglected.

It is noticeable, also, that this disposition to retain their children at home is not confined to the working classes,—it prevails considerably This is the cause reported to have been alleged by the parents of 12,067 absentee children in Manchester (Parliamentary Committee, 1852, Rev. C. Richson's evidence): but the motives to induce the parents to supply this reason rather than any other are so obvious that much caution is required before accepting their excuses. t The Self-imposed Taxation of the Working Classes. By the late G. R. Porter. amongst the classes far removed from indigence; and this suggests the inquiry, whether the same motives which produce neglect on the part of wealthy parents may not have an influence upon the conduct of those in humbler circumstances? The condition, too, of many of the *free* schools, where no payment is demanded of the scholar, seems to show that "poverty" is not an adequate explanation of the children's absence; for in many *free* schools, though located in the midst of populous neighbourhoods, the attendance of scholars is less numerous and much less constant than in schools which require a fee. The fact that free schools, well conducted, may be found half empty, while a multitude of uninstructed children who might enter them remain outside, seems inconsistent with the theory that *poverty* of the parents is the chief impediment to a sufficient school attendance.f

S. Criminal and 3. Unhappily there is, indeed, a much too numerous body of destitute *chil*dren?ate *dren,* who, having either lost their parents or been cast by them adrift, perpetually haunt large towns and cities, snatching a miserable and precarious subsistence as the fruit of vagrancy or crime. For these there seems but little chance of any useful education, unless the place of parents be supplied by other parties and some special measures undertaken with peculiar relation to this indigent and dangerous class. *Reformatory Schools* are therefore now with much zeal advocated; and the Government is urged to undertake towards all youthful criminals and vagrants the parental duty of pro-

viding them with wholesome education. With respect to actual convicted juvenile offenders, it is thought that the restraints of mental and moral discipline, while evidently more adapted than the present system to improve the character, would even be more efficacious as a *punishment*—being none the less restrictive of their liberty, perhaps more irksome as a task, and yet devoid of all those incident of physical infliction and untamed endurance which to the youthful criminal's depraved imagination give to unconquerable steadfastness in crime the semblance of heroic virtue. But, as to save such children from becoming criminal is better than to rescue them when fallen, the proposal comprehends the education also of such *unconvicted* children as, being parentless and destitute, have naturally no protectors but society. If these proposals be adopted, doubtless a gigantic step will have been taken towards the elevation of that section of the populace which hitherto has managed to escape all influence of moral agency, The education of the rest can probably be accomplished only by enlisting parents' sympathies and efforts in its favor.

4. Grand cause: 4. This, however, seems to be no easy task; for, after all allowances for proef parenCtтoiCe viously suggested causes of neglect, the great fact seems to be obtruded on our notice that the children's absence from, or very brief continuance at, school, is *mainly* owing to the slight esteem which parents have for the education itself which generally they might easily obtain. Beyond all question, much of this indifference results from a perception of the really trifling value of a great proportion of the education offered for their purchase; for the instances are not a few in which the improvement of a school is followed by increased Out of 654 children between three and fifteen years of ape belonging to the upper section of the middle classes, and resident in some of the more respectable squares and private streets of London, no less than 343 were not described in the Census schedules as being either at school or engaged in business. t See Evidence of Rev. W.

J. Kennedy before the Manchester and Salford Parliamentary Com mittee (1853)—

"1324. Do you think the manufacturing poor at all appreciate education generally P—Not to the fullest extent to which it is desirable; and to that I attribute the non-attendance of vast numbers of children.

"1325. Not from any want of means?—In some cases from want of means. I do not think to any very great extent from want of means: in fact 1 have made much inquiry on that subject, and I do not see how it can be when I find how many people are employed, and what the wages are that they are getting." attendance; but perhaps it principally flows from an idea, prevalent amongst the labouring classes, that instruction *beyond a certain point* can never be of any practical utility to those of their condition; for in general a parent, in whatever station, takes himself and his own social *status* as the standard up to which he purposes to educate his offspring: the nobility, the gentry, merchants, tradesmen, artifians, and agricultural labourers expect to see their children occupying just the same positions as themselves, and not unnaturally seek to qualify them for no higher duties. Hence it is that only those whose after-life is destined to be spent in intellectual exercises, as the pastime of an affluent leisure or the subject matter of professional activity, prolong their educational career beyond the elementary school period. The children of the mercantile community are thought to have completed their instruction when they have become adapted for the counting house—the sons of tradesmen when they have been fitted for apprentices—the sons of all engaged in manual industry as soon as they possess the manual strength and skill required for such pursuits. This, probably, is very false philosophy; but, practically, it is to be feared, the length and character of the education given in this country to the young are regulated more by a regard to its material advantage, as connected with their future physical condition, than by any wise appreciation of the benefits of knowledge in itself. It is hardly, therefore, matter for surprise, although undoubtedly it is for lamentation, that the working classes—seeing that the purely mental training which their children pass through in the present class of schools can rarely exercise an influence upon their future temporal prosperity, and having for some generations past been tutored not to look *beyond their station*—should esteem a thorough education of this character to be not worth the time and money needful for its acquisition. More, they may conceive, of *useful* information—useful to their children in their probable employments—may be learnt outside the school than in it; while, with reference to any other knowledge, it appears to them to be a vain expenditure of labour to acquire in youth the rudiments of arts and sciences which afterwards *must* be forgotten from the want of any stimulus or opportunity for their continued cultivation.

If in these remarks there is any considerable justice, we perceive at once the 'what are the educational position which it seems desirable and possible to reach, and the poffiespro" obstacles which lie across the path to such an elevation. What then, it may now be asked, are the means by which it is proposed, by those familiar with the subject, to remove these obstacles to progress?

Taking first the latest mentioned, it will doubtless be perceived what vast 1. Importance! of importance, as conducing to a longer school-attendance, is assignable to ctto?"6 *secondary* education. While it cannot be expected that a multitude of scholars should be found for a long time toiling along a weary road that leads to no desirable end of pleasure or of profit, it may reasonably be anticipated that, if ampler opportunities were furnished for the exercise, when school instruction may have ended, of the faculties which in the school were disciplined, and for the use and augmentation of the knowledge there acquired, a much more constant and prolonged attendance of their children at the elementary schools would be desired by parents, and encouraged. If, after reading and writing have been mastered, more inducements could be offered for the frequent application of these arts in daily life, unquestionably fewer persons would be This has occurred to several of our public writers, and was put with great force in the "Times" of Jan. 3I, 1854.

found unable, as at present, after some few years of manhood have elapsed, to read intelligibly, or to sign the marriage register except with marks. It is the goal in view that stimulates to perseverance in a tiresome course; but at present it must be, I fear, confessed, the working classes have no satisfactory reward to look to as the honourable end of their exertions. Much, no doubt, is now in process of accomplishment for giving them increased facilities for gaining information; and mechanics' institutions, reading clubs, and, lately, borough libraries, have been established; but, in spite of these and other efforts, the extent to which the labouring multitudes are found engaged in intellectual recreation is surprisingly and sadly insignificant. A vast work, therefore, evidently lies before us in the education of the *parents,* ere we can expect them to be earnest for the education of their children, and in preparing for the children now at school an after life of such abundant opportunities for selfimprovement that when *they* become the parents of succeeding children they may adequately value education from their own experience of its abiding fruits. Perhaps the most extravagant expenditure of funds and efforts in erecting and supporting and improving elementary schools would have but small efFect in lengthening school attendance, in comparison with that which would result from half the labour and expense applied to bring within the reach of those emerging from the school the means of cultivating as a pleasure intellectual occupations which in school they followed as a task. It is impossible to say how much of the intelligence and information of the mass of American citizens may be the consequence of their profusion of cheap literature; but certain is it that whatever tends to make the knowledge gained at school *available* in future years must exercise a potent influence in making school instruction more appreciated and demanded. Destitute of some such natural outlet, the pathway of the elementary school is little better than a *cul de sac.* 2. Elevation of the social *status* of parents.

Another means by which, it is suggested, parents may be interested in their children's more extended education, is to devolve upon them, so far as may with safety be attempted, various social duties and responsibilities. By thus conferring honourable obligations which require for their discharge some portion of capacity and information, strong incitements will, it is considered, be created to the exercise of much more intellectual activity; while the natural pride with which such privileges cannot fail to be regarded will excite parental jealousy for such an education of the children as would make them not unworthy of assuming in their turn the same agreeable responsibilities.f 3. Improvement of the primary schools.

These appear to be the most obvious methods of acting upon parents, apart from a compulsory intervention by the State; and this—although, perhaps, the most natural and logical conclusion from the arguments by which the duty of the State in the work of education is in general enforced—seems scarcely to be urged by any.—But, of course, contemporaneously with any efforts for the furtherance of *secondary* education as a means of securing a longer term of primary instruction, the improvement of the primary schools themselves must be effected as a measure of the utmost consequence. It has been shown already that—although, perhaps, the existing quantity of school accommodation is not far from adequate for the reception of as many children as could be expected to attend—a very considerable number of the present schools and teachers must be looked upon as inefficient. More especially is Mr. Whitworth's Report (New York Industrial Exhibition). t The " Congregational Board of Education" has adopted the expedient of associating parents in the management of the school, as a means of interesting them in the work of education, and impressing them with a conviction of its value. this the case with many of the private schools; which seem indeed, on this account, to he in course of gradual extinction, as the public schools increase from year to year in numbers and efficiency. But many of the public schools require considerable improvement, if the children are to be retained in them for a sufficient period. The school books and the school materials must be improved; the number of trained teachers must be much increased; the salaries of teachers must be raised; and more instruction must be given in a better form. Of these improvements educationists of every party admit, or rather proclaim, the need. The rapid development which, principally owing to the measures of the Privy Council, has been witnessed of the plan of Training Colleges for teachers, and the consequent revolution in the method and the subject matter of instruction in the primary schools, have operated to create in some degree a standard of efficiency towards which nearly every public school must now inevitably tend. When thus made thoroughly efficient, it is thought the schools can scarcely fail to attract the children who now stay away.—Upon the other hand, an apprehension seems to have been lately felt that this high training would defeat its object, if pursued without regard to those rude notions of the practical utility of education by which parents of the labouring classes regulate the length of children's school attendance; and, accordingly, some earnest counsels have been given that—while ably teaching reading, writing, history, geography—the importance to the working classes of a knowledge of the "common things" of life should not be overlooked.

It is not my purpose to form any estimate of the amount of work to be requlred'foTtho accomplished in order to obtain efficient schools for the 3,015,405 children efficient educawhom I have supposed to be in a position to attend. Sir James Kay ShuttlecWldren.000'009 worth computes that to provide an education, of the character contemplated by the Minutes of 1846, for 1,836,562 scholars in public schools of religious bodies, would require a total annual sum of 2,890,845/. (exclusive of the cost of new school *buildings);* or an *increase,* on the present annual expenditure, of 1,844,265/. No question can exist that, whatsoever be the standard of efficiency to which it may be deemed desirable to raise the public schools, a very heavy further outlay, both for new erections and for annual support, will be required. And scarcely less will be the outlay necessary to establish and sustain those further institutions for promoting *secondary* education, without which the extension of mere primary instruction cannot be of much avail. The questions which most urge themselves upon the public and upon the chief supporters of the cause of popular education are,—*the means by which this necessary outlay should be furnished.*

To obtain a definite idea of the value of the various suggestions offered in pre11" solution of this problem, it will be desirable to view the agencies by which amount of edu*existing* schools have been established and are now maintained. plied!1 '5 5UP The number of private schools has not at all increased since 1833 (when Lord Kerry's defective Return reported 29,141, with 732,449 scholars; the present number being.10,524, with 721,396 scholars), while the public schools have increased from 9,830 to 15,518, and the scholars in them from 544,698 to 1,422,982. The proportion of public schools to private which, in 1833, was as 34 to 100, had so increased, in 1851, that it was as 51 to 100; while the *scholars* in public schools, which in 1833, were only in the proportion of 74 to 100 in private schools; had increased, in 1851, to the proportion of 197 in the former to 100 in the latter.

EXISTING EDUCATIONAL AGENCIES. PRIMARY EDUCATION.

1. Day Schools.

According to the classification which has been adopted—chosen with the express design of showing the different

agencies by which our present educational establishments are founded and upheld—there are two great classes of schools, the Private and the Public. The former class includes all those sustained entirely by the payments of the scholars; the latter comprehends all those which gather *any portion* of their income from any source *besides* the scholars. There are 30,524 of the wholly self-supporting *private* schools, containing 721,396 scholars; and 15,518 of the aided *public* schools, containing 1,422,982 scholars.
s *Private Schools.*

Schools 'le PRIVATE Schools contain the bulk of the children of the middle and upper classes of society; for, with the exception of the Public Endowed Grammar Schools (and these almost exclusively for *boys),* there seems to be no other class of schools to which they could resort in any number. If the previous distribution of the private schools according to their character (see page 29) can be accepted as approximately accurate, it will be found that (as the ascertained average of scholars to each of the schools there called "inferior" is about 15) the total number of scholars in about 15,000 schools which probably are adapted for the children of the working classes would be somewhere near 225,000, leaving a residue of nearly 500,000 to represent the children of the middle and upper classes. To these there cannot, apparently, be added more than 50,000 as likely to be found in any of the public schools; thus making the total number of the children of the middle and upper classes at school in March 1851 to be 550,000. This it will be seen gives only an average of 54 years' schooling for the children of these classes, on the assumption that they constitute *a fourth* of the total number between three and fifteen (viz.:—a fourth of 4,908,696 = 1,227,174). But, as 50,000 more appear to be in regular receipt of adequate instruction, under professional teachers *at home,* the average period for the whole would be raised to six years. It has generally been assumed, by writers on the subject, that as much as *eight* years out of the twelve is devoted by these classes to the education of their children, an assumption which can be supported only by concluding either that the proportion of these classes to the total population must be less than a fourth, or else that the amount of home education is much larger than the Census Tables shew. The result which will be arrived at probably is—that an *eight* years' average is too high—that the children of these classes must, in many cases, be retained at home till five or six years old (perhaps receiving education from the elder members of their families)—and that the actual period which they pass at school, or under regular professional teachers at home, cannot be much more than *six* years. This seems to show that neglect of school instruction is not confined to the working classes; and indeed, when the charge for education at such schools as alone are suitable for children of the middle classes is remembered, it must be apparent that the plea of "poverty," as a cause of non-attendance,

Two great classes of Day Schools —
Private and
Public.
In the calculations of the Report I assume a *six* years' average *at school,* independent of home tuition. This will allow for the possibility of any omissions in the enumeration of schools for these classes.
must be often much more applicable to parents of respectable position, though with limited income, than to those on whose behalf it is most usually urged. Good schools, on reasonable terms, for children of the middle classes, are perhaps more needed than new National or British Schools.

It seems improbable that private schools will become less numerously attended than at present. The number of *schools,* no doubt, will gradually decrease, as superior schools, both private and public, are established; but, while many of the very small inferior schools thus disappear, it is likely that superior new private schools will occupy their place to even a greater extent than will new public schools. For the system of "common schools," in which the children of the different classes of society are educated all together, is not likely to succeed in England, where the tone of social feeling is decisively opposed to such a democratic intermixture. If the children of the middle and upper classes constitute about a fourth part of the whole number of children (4,928,176) between 3 and 15, and if they, on an average, spend six years out of the twelve at school, there will always be upwards of 500,000 either in private schools or in the public endowed schools, but principally in the former. And the spirit of independence which exists to a very considerable extent among the prosperous and provident members of the working class will probably for some time yet to come keep up the demand for a certain additional number of private schools. It cannot, therefore, be anticipated that a larger proportion than *two thirds* of the total school accommodation requisite (whatever that may be) will be found in *public* schools: a third of the whole will always, we may venture to assert, continue to be maintained entirely and exclusively by the scholars.
Public Schools.
Who are the parties likely to co-operate with the scholars in providing the Public remaining two thirds will be seen by a reference to the state of things with Schools respect to existing Public Schools. These, with a view to this inquiry, have been separated in the Table into four subordinate classes, which, though not invariably distinct, are yet perhaps sufficiently defined to aid this object. These four classes are as follows: I. Schools supported by General or Local Taxation.
II. Schools supported by Endowments.
III. Schools supported by Religious Bodies. IV. Other Public Schools.

It is obvious that some of these classes intermix to greater or less extent with others; since some schools are found to be supported by a mixture of endowments and subscriptions. The auxiliary support supplied by the scholars themselves, being generally common to all the classes, has not been considered to affect the distribution. The criterion by which the schools maintained by a combination of endowments and subscriptions have been placed to Class II. or Clas3 III., has been the *preponderance* of the receipts from one or the other of these sources. But a method has been found of showing the precise extent to which the numbers are affected by the adoption of this arbitrary test. Class IV. consists of a number of schools, of a rather miscellaneous character, which could not be referred to either of the other classes; principally schools supported by a general contemporaneous philanthropy, not acting through the medium of any religious body. Subject to these explanations, the following is the aspect of our public day schools, classified as thus described:— For a further explanation of tho plan on which the classification was conducted, see the

As already intimated, some of the schools here placed with Class II. (because their *chief* support, apart from school-pence, is derived from endowments,) nevertheless receive a *portion* of their income from religious bodies; and, on the other hand, some of the schools here placed with Class III. (because their *chief* support, apart from school-pence, is derived from religious bodies,) nevertheless receive a. *portion* of their income from endowments. The extent of this intermixture is, that in Class II. are included 2,113 schools (with 139,935 scholars) which are, in a subordinate degree, supported by Religious Bodies; while in Classes III. and IV. are included 896 schools (with 111,297 scholars) which are, in a subordinate degree, supported by Endowments. (See *post,* Supplements I., II., III. to Table B. pp. 92-93.)

Class I. Schools SupPorted By General Or Local TaxaTion.

Proceeding now to the details of these classes,

I. The following is a more particular account of the 610 schools which compose Class I.:—

Table 8.

This Table does not contain any estimate for the 107 public schools which made no returns as no means exist of satisfactorily distributing them amongst the four classes.

These, indeed, do not represent the whole of the schools supported in a measure by *taxation;* for the Government is now expending as much as 60,000/. per annum in support of schools and teachers; but as this amount (except what is applied to workhouse schools) is given in aid of larger contributions by Religious Bodies, it has seemed advisable to include the schools receiving it amongst those in Class III.
II. The schools supported by Endowments have been distinguished into Class II. only *two* subordinate sections, viz., (1.) The *Endowed Collegiate and Grammar* Poetedbtp" *Schools,* and (2.) *Other Endowed Schools;* the former consisting of all that are Endowments. either distinctly so described in the returns, or evidently so from the character Number, of the instruction given; the latter consisting of all that, being endowed, are neither described as grammar schools, nor appear to be such from the subjectmatter of the teaching. Table 9. exhibits the number of each class of school and the number of scholars. Table 9.

But this, as before mentioned, does not show the whole number of schools supported *in any degree* by endowments. Some of the schools in Classes. III. and IV. are also to some extent endowed. The particulars of these, are shown in Supplement III. to Table B. *(post,* Summary Tables, p. 93); from which it will be seen that, if it be desired to ascertain the total number of schools receiving endowments, *of whatever amount,* there must be added to the above 2,559 "Other Endowed Schools" 869 of the schools principally supported by religious bodies, containing 107,184 scholars, and 27 of the other public subscription schools, containing 4,113 scholars. The result will be that the total number of schools receiving any amount of endowment will be 4,021, containing 317,576 scholars. On the other hand, a certain number (viz., 2,113) of the 2,559 schools here placed to Class II. are also in part supported by religious bodies. (See Supplement I. to Table B. *post* p. 92.)

The amount and sources of the income of the above schools may perhaps be Income, roughly guessed from the following statement of the income of 1,911 of the number; but as the income from endowments varies so extensively, and as no facilities exist for ascertaining whether they were the richest or the poorest schools which gave no information, it has not been deemed advisable to construct an estimate for the total number based upon the figures which apply to the 1,911.

This gives a very inadequate idea of the annual value of endowments for the purpose of education. Lord Brougham estimated the amount at 500,000/. per annum, and recent writers have expressed a similar opinion. A great amount of this is misappropriated; hut it is to be expected that the new Board established under the Act of last session will recover to its proper uses no inconsiderable portion.

size of Endow-The *size* of individual endowments may be seen from the following statement mints. 0f the number of schools receiving, each of them, endowments within the various limits of the under-mentioned scale:—

This Table includes all schools supported *in any degree* by endowments, whether they have been referred to Class II. or Class III.

Antiquity of The endowed schools represent the movements of past ages in the work of

Schools. education. Many of them are of great antiquity, and most of them had their origin before the 19th century. The following Table shows the various periods in which the present schools were founded:— See chapter on Charitable Trusts in Sir James K. Shuttleworth's work on Public Education.

The precise dates of the most ancient of existing schools are these, A.D. 1216, 1268, 1284, 1350, 1363, 13/9, 1383, 1393, 1394, 1400, 1418, 1441, 1444, 1449, 1450, 1472, 1473, 1482, 1483, 1484, 1487, 1490, 1495, 1497, 1499.

Of course instruction is carried further in this cla3s of schools than in any other, and more scholars will be found whose studies reach the higher branches. Table 13. will show the actual state of things in 2,626 of the endowed schools which compose Class II. As the greater number of the "Other Endowed Schools" are, in truth, Denominational Schools (though supported chiefly by endowments), the comparison between them and the Collegiate and Grammar Schools will show the difference between the instruction imparted in the latter and that supplied in the mass of public day schools for the poor. The facts relate to the instruction given to *boys.*

Table 13.

The action of Religious Bodies in the matter of popular education has Class III.

throughout the present century been powerful, extensive, and increasing; and Schools Stjp the present result of their exertions constitutes by far the most important and Religious conspicuous feature of our educational position. It is scarcely possible to avoid Bodies. being deeply impressed by the accumulated evidence we now apparently possess of the inexhaustible resources and illimitable enterprises of religious zeal. The erected twenty thousand places of religious worship—founded three and twenty thousand Sunday schools, containing two and a quarter millions of scholars— and brought within the compass of its Christian charity the utmost regions of the globe—the fact that this insatiable benevolence has also almost wholly reared, and is now in greater part sustaining, upwards of *ten thousand* Day Schools, in which more than *a million* children of the poorer classes are from day to day instructed—cannot but excite a very lively sense, not only of the obligations under which the country lies to the workings of religious principle, but also of the vast extent to which in future all the institutions of popular education must be necessarily pervaded by religious influence.

Some difficulty is experienced in stating any precise figures as representing the number of schools which may be fairly said to be " supported by religious bodies "; since, as already mentioned, schools in many cases are maintained by a combination of endowments and subscriptions in nearly equal proportions. In the present classification, where the chief resources of a school consist of permanent endowments, it has been considered best to place it in a separate class of " Endowed Schools," although another portion of its income may consist of contributions from a certain religious body, and although the management of the school may be in the hands of that religious body. The adoption of this course appeared to be desirable, because of an essential difference between endowments and subscriptions; the latter indicating an amount of really existing religious zeal—whereas the former cannot in the same way be regarded as evincing any present action of religious sentiment, and are often liable, as times and circumstances change, to be appropriated to the sustentation of a different faith from that professed by their donors. The rule, undoubtedly, is somewhat arbitrary, and therefore care has been taken to supply the means of making any other classification, if this should be esteemed unsatisfactory. Thus, *two* views can be given of the schools connected with religious bodies; one upon the basis now described, and the other on the supposition that if *any* portion of the aid proceeds from religious bodies *they* should be considered the supporters. The one view is shown in Table B. (page 91.), and the other in Supplement II. to Table B. (page 92). According to the former, there are 10,595 schools (containing 1,048,851 scholars) which may be fairly awarded to religious bodies as contributing the greater portion of their income; while, according to the latter, there are 12,708 schools (containing 1,188,786 scholars) to which religious bodies furnish *some* pecuniary aid, and all of which are subject to their management.

And the extent to which religious bodies are assuming the control of popular education is continually and rapidly increasing. This will be in some degree made manifest by the. following statement of the periods during which the 10,595 existing schools, composing Class HI., were founded:—

This, of course, does not display the whole number of schools existing at each of the periods named; but only the number which, existing then, have survived until the present time. Some, no doubt, which were in operation formerly, have since become extinct; and many more have been enlarged, or superseded by new buildings, and most probably, when this has been the case, the *later* date has been the one supplied. But all allowance proper upon these accounts will not deprive of its significance the remarkable fact that within the last ten years no fewer than 4,6'04 school buildings (either wholly additional to the previous supply, or larger and better substitutes for others,) have been raised by religious bodies. The number of scholars in these 4,604 schools is probably about 450,000. Towards the cost of erecting or enlarging a certain number (about 2,000) of these 4,604 schools the State has granted, through the Committee of Privy Council, about 320,000/.; *f* whilst the total cost of the whole 4,604 may be estimated at about 2,500,000/.

The cost at which the schools of religious bodies are supported may, perhaps, be gathered from the statements as to income which were furnished with respect to 5,761 of the number. Accurate returns, however, of financial matters are proverbially difficult to be procured. In dealing with the Census returns, the utmost care has been expended to extract reliable results; and the aim has consequently been, rather to select a considerable number of undoubtedly correct and full returns than to accumulate a mass of figures which, in consequence of obvious omissions and inaccuracies in some of the returns, would afford no safe materials for inference. The total income, for the year 1850, of the 5,761 schools, from which sufficiently authentic statements were received, was 459,627/. The number of scholars in these schools being 634,134, this niakes the average annual expense of each to be 14s. *6d.* If it can be assumed that the income of the remaining 4,834 schools was the same per scholar as that of the above 5,761, the total annual income of the whole 10,595 schools in Class III. having 1,048,851 scholars, will be 760,218/.; and if the 2,113 schools belonging to religious bodies—which have been placed amongst "Endowed Schools" in Class II.—be taken into account, the total income will be 960,188/. for 1,188,786 scholars. The following Table (14) shows the sources of this income:

Annual cost of the schools of Religious Bodies.

The number of Teachers is returned for 8,232 of the schools of religious Number of bodies. In these there are 44,167 teachers (22,176 males and 21,991 females) Slfof Eelithus composed, vifi., 14,858 *general teachers* (5,902 masters and 8,956 mis-gious Bodies. tresses), 8,312 *paid monitors and pupil-teachers* (4,418 males and 3,894 females), and 20,997 *unpaid teachers* (11,856 males and 9,141 females). These teachers instruct 875,238 scholars (484,112 males and 391,126 females). If it be That is, upon the supposition that each of the 4,604 schools contains upon an average the same number of scholars as did each of the 10,595 which in the aggregate were found to have 1,049,8511 but the probability is that they contained more.

assumed that the proportions of teachers to scholars is the same in the remaining 2,363 schools as in the above 8,232, the total number of teachers, and of each kind, in the schools of religious bodies, contained in Class III., will be shown in Table 15.

Table 15.

The *remuneration* of teachers is the least satisfactory portion of the Census returns; the omissions being many, and the ambiguities not few. From what can be gathered from the facts returned for the two counties of Lancashire and Lincolnshire, it appears that the average emolument of *masters* is *55l.* and of. *mistresses, 3l.*

Course of instruction in the schools of Religious Bodies.

Particular Denominations.

The course of instruction followed in the schools of religious bodies has been indicated m the case of 8,959 schools (out of 10,380) in which boys are taught, and in the case of 8,891 schools (out of 10,328) in which girls are taught. The number of schools, out of an average 100, in which instruction is afforded in certain subjects, will be seen in Table 16.

Table 16.

When we come to analyse this class into its constituent elements, it will be found that the schools of the Church of England form 81 per cent. and her scholars 76 per cent. of the whole. If the mixed endowed and subscription schools, referred in the Tables to the former, be included, the proportions will be yet more favourable, being 83 per cent. of the schools and 78 per cent. of the scholars. The actual number of each belonging to the several religious bodies will be seen in Table 17., which is constructed so as to show the numbers upon either mode of reckoning, whether or not those schools should be regarded as supported by religious bodies whose income from endowment exceeds the income from subscriptions.

i

From this it will be manifest that not only has popular education, in this country, been promoted mainly by a *religious* influence, but that it is nowbecoming rapidly a matter of *denominational* activity. This tendency, so far as the Dissenters are concerned, has only recently been evidenced; for schools upon the *British* system (which discourages sectarian teaching) satisfied their wants till about ten years ago. The controversies of that period, however, when it seemed to the Dissenters that the Government designed to place too much of the education of the poor in the hands of the Established Church, produced very great exertions on the part of the various bodies to counteract this supposed Not otherwise denned in the Betums.

t This line represents only the British Schools which are not returned as being connected with any particular denomination. Many British schools are included in this Table amongst those belonging to spectic religious bodies. The total number altogether is, on tho first view, 832, containing 123,015 scholars, and, upon the second view, 857, containing 123,496 scholars. *a* design; and the schools which were erected as a consequence of these exertions naturally were connected with the sects hy which they were originated—to whose interests, indeed, they were intended as a sort of bulwark. How far this denominational action is henceforward to proceed is a very important question. It is clear, however, that Dissenting bodies are not likely to be represented in proportion to their numbers by the day schools which their small comparative 'wealth will enable them to raise and carry on—exposed, too, as many of them must be, to the competition of schools aided by the public funds. An interesting problem, therefore, is before us,—" How is the education of poor children of Dissenting parents to be provided for, in order to secure religious liberty?" At first sight it appears inevitable that in course of time the mass of the population, educated of necessity in Church of England schools, must gradually return to that community; but, in opposition to this natural anticipation, is the curious fact, that—while for many years past at least *four fifths* of all the children who have passed through public schools must have been instructed in the schools of the Church of England—concurrently with this, a very considerable augmentation has (according to the tables of Religious Worship) been proceeding in the number of Dissenters; so that now they number very nearly half of the total population. This appears to prove, that either the education given by the Church has been administered on very tolerant and liberal principles, or else the sectarian and doctrinal instruction of the day school is extremely ineffective in comparison with those religious influences which the scholar meets elsewhere.

Chttbch Ob T8 great educational organ of the Church Of England is the National

NaHonaSociety Society, founded in 1811, and incorporated by Royal Charter in 1817. Its annual income from subscriptions, and other contributions paid directly to the General Fund of the Society has averaged, during the last four years, nearly 11,0007. per annum. Besides this, the Welsh Education Fund of the Society amounts to nearly 3,000/. a year, and there are other funds, at times considerable in amount, raised for particular objects. Jn addition to these, at various times since 1823, a Royal Letter (now triennial) has been issued, sanctioning parochial collections in favour of the Society. The amounts collected at the several periods hitherto have been as follows:— Amount collected. Year of Letter. £ 1823--28,292 1832--23,535 1837--24,838   1840--30,002   1843--32,602

Connected with the Central Institution, local boards of education have, since 1839, been founded in nearly every diocese. The income of these boards is probably about 20,000/. annually. The Central Board makes grants in aid of local contributions for the purpose of erecting schools to be conducted in accordance with the charter; though its principle and practice have always been to abstain from interference with the managers of schools thus built. It also furnishes from its depository schoolbooks and apparatus as a means of promoting the efficiency of local schools. It has also under its immediate management five training colleges, supported in whole or in part from the funds of the Society, which now send out annually above 270 teachers. Most of these institutions are of recent origin, though one has been in operation under various forms since

Amount collected. Year of Letter. £ 1846--27,191 1849--24,863 1852 (up to Mar. 1854)-22,810 The " Church Education Society" was not in existence at the time of the Census; having been formed as recently as May 1863. Its income, to the 31st March 1864, was about 4,800.
the first establishment of the Society in 1811. An active movement for procuring Diocesan Training schools was commenced by the Society in 1838; and there are now as many as 20 such institutions united to the Parent Society in different parts of England and Wales.

In connexion with several of the local boards diocesan inspectors have been appointed. There are also three training colleges belonging to the Church of England unconnected with the National Society.

The number of trained teachers annually sent out from these institutions may be estimated at about 400 masters and 250 mistresses. This number includes those given above as trained directly by the National Society.

In 1846, the Society undertook an extensive investigation into the state of Church education in the country; and the facts collected-showed that the number of Church day schools then existing was 17,015, with 955,865 scholars. Of this number of schools 6,798 were reported as connected with the Society, containing 526,754 scholars. The numbers according to the present Census are, 10,555 schools and 929,474 scholars; of which 3,995 schools, having 493,876 scholars, are said to be National schools. The difference between the two statements is explained in part by the different mode of computation adopted—the Society's statistics reckoning a school for boys and a school for girls to be two schools, although in one building, whereas in the Census tables they have only been counted as *one*. So, too, as to scholars—the Society's inquiry included children in Church *dame* schools, whereas such in the Census tables are referred to *private* schools. It is very possible, too, that schools may be in connexion with the Society though not described so in the returns; especially as, up to Christmas 1853, there were, on the books of the National Society, 10,193 schools in direct union.

The large majority of Church of England schools now erected are aided both by the Committee of Council on Education and by the National Society. All such schools are secured by a trust deed in which one of certain Management Clauses, proposed by the Committee of Council, is inserted. To these clauses the National Society makes no objection; indeed it is asserted, the great principle involved in them,—that there should be managers besides the Parochial Clergy—has always been distinctly recognized by that Society. The National Society withdrew its recommendation, at one time given, of these clauses, on the ground that the adoption of them was made compulsory by the Committee of Council on all promoters of schools; but aid from the Society has never been withheld in any case on account of the adoption of those clauses.

The following Table (18.) shows the operations of the Church in the various counties, and in the more extensive towns of England. After due allowance for the education received in private schools and other public schools than those of the Church of England, it may probably be said that a proportion of six or seven scholars in Church schools to 100 of the population at all ages would express a satisfactory amount of Church instruction. In *towns* a less proportion must be looked for than in rural districts, in consequence of the larger demand for juvenile labour. The Table shows how far, and in what places, this assumed   proportion   has   been reached:—

The activity of the Church in recent years in the work of education will be seen by reference to the following statement of the dates at which existing schools$X$ were founded; bearing in mind the qualifications previously mentioned as being necessary to be made (pp. 46-47.):— Before 1801 1801-1811 1811-1821
1821-1831
1831-1841
1841-1851
Not stated

Total Excluding schools where the endowment exceeds the amount of subscription.

t The limits taken for these towns are those of the *Municipal Boroughs,* except in the cases of Brighton and London—the former referring to the Parliamentary Borough, and the latter to the entire Metropolis. t *Excluding* schools tho chief support of which is from *endowments.*

The amount and sources of income of Church schools are returned for 4,546 schools, containing 472,372 scholars.

The total amount for these schools is stated at 341,752*l.* for the year 1850; which gives an average income of 14s. 5d. per scholar. The sources of this income were—*Permanent Endowment,* 13,240*l.*; *Voluntary Contributions,* 179,765*l.*; *Grants from Government,* 18,132*l.*; *Payments by Scholars,* 103,264*l.*; *Other sources,* 27,351*l.*—If this proportion were applied to the whole number of Church schools and scholars in Class III., the total amount of annual income would be 579,875*l.*; to which must be added about 182,867*l.* for the endowed Church schools in Class II.; making an aggregate of 762,742*l.* This, however, must be a very inadequate view of the amount raised by the Church of England in support of elementary education; for the returns published by the National Society in 1846-7 shew a total amount of 874,948*l.*

Of the various religious bodies, other than the Established Church, which IiroEPEJrdEitTS support Denominational day schools, the Congregationalists occupy at Motasbis" present the first place with reference to the number of schools and scholars thus maintained. In the Census returns it seems that 453 schools were expressly stated to belong to this denomination; 185 of which were "British" schools. The total number of scholars in these 453 schools was 50,186 (see Supplement II. to Table B.) This, however, will not completely represent the efforts made by Congregationalists; as, doubtless, no inconsiderable part of the contributions which support the purely undenominational British schools proceeds from members of this community.

Indeed, as already hinted,f separate denominational action by Dissenters generally in the work of education is of very recent origin: that of the Congregational body commenced in 1843. Prior to this period the Independents, though undoubtedly warm friends of education, seldom founded schools in immediate connexion with their congregations: their support was given to schools conducted on the British system, the essential features of which—the daily reading of the Bible, and the exclusion of all special creeds and catechisms—seemed to secure at once religious education and religious liberty. But when, in 1843, their disapproval of the measure of Education proposed by Government impelled Dissenters to a more extensive effort than before to establish day schools, the Congregational body came to the resolution, that, not for the purpose of sectarian teaching, but as a means of giving greater vigour to the movement, it was most desirable that their own efforts should be made in their denominational capacity. This resolve was taken first at a meeting of the Congregational Union J held at Leeds in October 1843, and was afterwards confirmed at a special representative meeting of 170 ministers and 151 lay delegates held in London in the subsequent December. At these meetings it was also deliberately agreed that the efforts of the Congregationalists should be entirely *voluntary*—altogether independent of the State.§ The Independents or Congregationalists, according to the Census of Religious Worship, have 3,244 chapels and stations, containing accommodation for 1,067,760 persons. The estimated number of attendants at these places of worship every Sunday is stated at 793,142.

t See *ante* page 15. t The " Congregational Union of England and 'Wales" is a delegated conference of ministers and laymen, meeting twice a year for consultation on the state and prospects of the body, and for such co-operative action as can be adopted for its welfare without violation of the principle of independency. The constitution of the Union, therefore, provides that it " shall not in any ease assume a legislative authority or become a court of appeal." There is no doubt, however, that its resolutions in the matter of education express the sentiments of nearly the wholo body.

§ The resolutions of the Leeds Meeting were as follow:—

"That the subject of general education, in itself of great and vital moment, has acquired at the present juncture, in the judgment of this meeting, especial importance, as the result of the successful resistance of the friends of religious liberty to the partial and arbitrary measure proposed by Government in the recent session of Parliament; because the question in this country is uow, more than ever, seen to be closely associated with differences of theological opinion on points of vital moment, and with claims,.on the one hand, to ecclesiastical domination, and, on the other, to religious freedom and social equality."

"That without pronouncing a decided opinion on the propriety of Government interference in the education of the people, this meeting entertains the greatest doubts whether any compulsory

The rejection by the Congregationalists of State assistance to their schools results in chief from their well-known fundamental principle, that public money ought in no case to be given to provide *religions teaching.* And whether it be in the pulpit or in the schoolroom that religious doctrine is expounded or religious influence exerted, matters little in their view: that religious teaching should be wholly unsupported by the State is the unanimous conviction of the Congregational body. Some, indeed, appear to consider that by separating the religious from the secular instruction of the day schools public money might be taken for the latter without any violation of their principles; but the advocates of his opinion, though respectable, are not numerous, and the great majority of Independents hold that such a separation would be highly detrimental to religious education—that religion *must* form part, and no subordinate part, of daily training—and that therefore Congregationalists are utterly precluded from receiving any aid from Parliamentary grants. The Minutes of Council of 1846 appear to have rather strengthened than diminished their objection; since, they say, not only by those minutes is the public money given for religious teaching, but for the teaching of contradictory religions.—It is, too, from the members of this body that the chief support is given to that argument for voluntary education which is founded on political and economic principles; regarding education as a matter not within the proper range of Governmental agency, and likely to be rather hindered than assisted by its interference.f

The Congregationalists, thus resolved to trust entirely to their own resources, raised at once considerable sums of money for the purpose of establishing schools, and formed a Central Board.

The "Congregational Board of Education/' aS the central body is denominated, has an annual income of about 2,900/. Its principal objects are—the training of teachers, inspection, assistance to local schools, and the general improvement of the system of education. At first, its teachers were trained by the British and Foreign School Society; but when that Society accepted public money, separate training institutions were established which were afterwards united at Homerton College, an establishment previously devoted, for more than a hundred years, to the training of students for the ministry among the Independents. On the removal of the institution for ministerial training to New College, London, the premises of Homerton College were obtained by the Congregational Board of Education, and adapted to their present purpose, at a total cost of 12,000/., including the erection of model or practising schools. J To secure the religious character of the teachers, it is provided that no candidate for admission into any normal school connected with the Board shall be eligible who is not in communion with some Christian church, or whose Christian character is not otherwise well attested. The system of training adopted in this college interference can take place without establishing principles and precedents dangerous to civil and religious liberty, inconsistent with tho rights of industry, and superseding the duties of parents and of churches; while all tho plans of national education by the agency of Government, suggested of late years, have been very objectionable, either to the friends of the Established Church or to the dissenting bodies. This meeting, therefore, concludes, without despondency or regret, that both the general and the religious education of the people of England must bo chiefly provided and conducted by the voluntary efforts of the various denominations of Christians." See the resolution passed at the London Meeting, in 1843. "Resolved, That this Meeting, utterly repudiating, on the strongest grounds of Scripture and conscience, the receipt of money raised by taxation, and granted by Government, for sustaining the Christian religion, feels bound to apply this principle no less to the work of religious education; and, considering that the education given by the Congregational Churches must be religious, advises most respectfully but most earnestly that no Government aid be received by Congregational Churches for schools established in their own connexion; and that all funds confided to the disposal of the Central Committee in aid of schools be granted only to schools sustained entirely by voluntary contributions." Meeting of 18 and 14 Dec. 1843.

+ See the argument of the voluntary party upon this view, *post* page 76. *t* In 1853 the college is reported to have had 49 students, and the practising schools 269 children. It is also stated that the Board has trained altogether 166 teachers (71 male and 95 female), and that the average salary of the male teachers who had been appointed to schools was embodies the principal features of that which is generally known as the "Glasgow system," (from having been so successfully pursued by Mr. David Stow at Glasgow,) with modifications introduced by the principal of Homerton College, the Rev. W. J. Unwin, M.A.

Congregationalists are careful to distinguish between a denominational course of action, and a system of sectarian teaching. Their resolve to act as a religious body apart, in general, from other bodies, is, they say, adopted purely for the sake of more efficient and harmonious action, and of the greater opportunities it gives for enlisting in the cause of education the sympathies of the various churches. But admission to their schools is unrestricted; and, while the education given is based upon evangelical principles, no special catechisms are introduced, nor is any other mode of proselytism sanctioned.

The amount of money raised from December 1843 to April 1853 appears to be as near as possible 160,000 (exclusive of the annual sums devoted to the *maintenance* of schools). The following statement of the dates at which existing congregational schools were built or enlarged will show to some extent the effect of this activity:

Number of existing Schools DATE; established.

The Wesleyan Methodistsj, according to the Census returns, have con-'wesleyak nected with them 381 day schools, with 41,144 scholars. But to these numbers Methodists. some addition should be made, in order to see the actual extent of Wesleyan educational provision, on account of *British* schools which are often partly supported by Wesleyans in localities where they themselves are not sufficiently numerous or wealthy to have schools exclusively their own.

It is only within comparatively recent years that Wesleyan Methodists have originated any organized denominational efforts for establishing and supporting day schools. John Wesley, indeed, was an ardent friend of popular education; and no inconsiderable portion of his long existence and gigantic labours was devoted to this object §; but, with rare exceptions, all the efforts which, in

" The education given inschools connected with this Board shall be conducted on evangelical views of religion: neither the learning of any denominational formulary, nor attendance at any particular place of worship, shall be a condition of admittance into them: any committee of a school, or of an auxiliary, will not be acting contrary to the rules of this Board by admitting members of other denominations to share in either the support or management of such schools; and no school so constituted shall be on that account less eligible to receive any needful help from the Board." t This is the number referred to Class III. in the Tables. Thero are twenty-two others which have beenplaced in Class II. as being *principally* supported by endowments.

t The Wesleyan Methodists of the Original Connexion have, according to the Census Export on Religious Worship, 6,579 places of worship, with accommodation for 1,444,580 persons.

§ It is incidentally mentioned in his journal that in 1739 he had begun to build a school in the middle of Kingswood (Bristol) for the children of the colliers. Subsequently he had children taught in his own house. He then engaged two schoolmasters, the expense being partly defrayed by voluntary contributions. One institution, called an " Orphan House," was next established in Newcastle; and in 1748 he founded an improved middle class grammar school at Kingswood, which is still existing in a somewhat altered character. He urged his preachers to make education sometimes the special topic of their discourses. His literary labours, too, wero very considerable; and cheap editions of good works anpear to have had their attraction then no less than How. Grammars of the English, French, Latin, and Greek languages—abridged histories of Borne, of England, and of the Christian Church—a Compendium of Natural t'hilo following his example, Wesleyan Methodists put forth for the promotion of day school education in this country, were combined with similar exertions on the part of other bodies; and the children of the poorer classes of Wesleyan parents were instructed either in British or Church of England schools. No formal action by the Conference was taken until 1833; and then it was only in the shape of a recommendation that schools should be established wherever practicable. In 1836, however, a committee was appointed on the subject, which reported the existence of 31 schools; and in 1837 was formed an "Educational Committee" (consisting of 15 ministers and 15 laymen, with treasurer and secretary,) charged with the general supervision of all matters relating to Wesleyan education. The stimulus applied by this committee seems to have been effectual; for in 1840 the number of schools had increased to 101, having 8,193 scholars. And about this period, being aided by a grant of 5,000/. from the Centenary Fund , the committee first began the work of training efficient teachers—sending them, with that design, to the Glasgow Normal Seminary. In 1843 a fund of 20,000/. was raised, and half the proceeds of an annual collection was appropriated to the use of the committee. This has now been superseded by a special collection (annually made in April), which is henceforth to be considered as the Connexional income for educational purposes. Last year this income amounted to 3,327/. The total expenditure of the committee from 1840 to January 1854 has been 64,133/. Of this amount, *5,5921.* was disbursed in grants to 246 schools, erected within that period or fitted up at a cost of 61,540/.; 10,438/. was expended in training 448 students at Glasgow; and the residue was principally devoted to the establishment of the "Wesleyan Training Institution" at Westminster, which was opened in 1851, having cost about 40,000/. (of which the Committee of Privy Council granted 7,600/.)

The influence of the controversies of 1843 and 1846 was not unfelt by the Wesleyan body. The projected legislation of the former period created much alarm, and gave a surprising impulse to the work of providing day schools. It was then proposed to build within the next seven years as many as 700 schools; and, although this scheme has not been wholly realised, a very considerable addition has been made. The proof of this appears in the following statement of the dates at which existing Wesleyan day schools were established, recollecting that the definition of a " school" adopted in these Tables may be different from that contemplated when 700 schools were spoken of:—

Total--363 f sophy—portable editions of Milton and Young—a collection (in 50 volumes) of Treatises on Practical Divinity by Puritan and Episcopalian authors—these all owed their origin to his fieal for useful knowledge among the people. Probably the very magnitude of his fame in a more exalted sphere of labour has prevented an adequate recognition of his claim to honour as an earlyas well as an earnest champion of popular enlightenment.

The Centenary of Wesleyan Methodism was celebrated in 1839, when, as a token of their gratitude for the benefits which the system had conferred upon them, the Weslcyans raised a fund of no less amount than 216,000?., which was appropriated to the establishment of two theological institutions, in Lancashire and at Richmond—the purchase of the " Centenary Hall and Mission House" in Bishopsgate Street—the provision of a missionary ship—the discharge of chapel debts—and the augmentation of the incomes of the various Methodist societies. t This number is exclusivo of 18 schools which are principally supported by endowments.

The total amount of money raised by Wesleyan Methodists for education since 1840 cannot be less than 207,000/. The discussion which ensued upon the publication of the Minutes of Council of 1846 resulted in the acceptance by Wesleyans of assistance from the Parliamentary grant. Indeed, this body has never, at any time, objected to the *principle* of State-support to religious teaching; and having obtained such modifications of the Minutes as removed the difficulties which, on other grounds, they felt, they saw no reason why they should refuse assistance which appeared to them to be unclogged with harsh conditions.

Wesleyan day schools are conducted, nearly universally, upon the training system founded by Mr. Stow of Glasgow. As already stated, 448 of their teachers were actually trained at Glasgow; and all the distinctive features of the system are displayed in the Westminster Institution, which is said to be one of the most complete in the country, having five practising and model schools (with space for 1,000 children), and accommodation (fully occupied at present) for 100 students. Thirty-four of the present students are Queen's Scholars. The fee is 15/. per annum, and the usual term of study is two years.

The elementary schools are managed by local committees, two thirds of which are always to consist of Wesleyan Methodists, and must include the ministers of the circuit. The schools are to be of a distinctively religious character: the daily instruction is to be commenced and concluded with prayer; choral psalmody, from the Wesleyan Hymn Book, is to be a daily exercise; the Bible and the Wesleyan Catechism are to be in daily use; no doctrines contrary to Wesley's "Notes on the New Testament" are to be taught; and on Sundays the children are to be conducted to Wesleyan Chapels. These regulations are, however, not to apply to children whose parents may upon religious grounds object. A clause to this effect forms part of the Model Trust Deed sanctioned by the Conference.

The income of 243 day schools is stated in the returns, out of the total number of 363 which have been referred to Class III. The aggregate income for the year 1850 for these 243 schools (containing 29,814 scholars on the books) was 23,866/., obtained from the following sources: *permanent endowment,* 48/.; *voluntary contributions,* 8,181/.; *grants from Government,* 1,862/.; *payments by scholars,* 12,622/.; *other sources,* 1,153/. This gives an average income for each scholar of 15s. 3d. per annum.

Since March 1851, when the Census was taken, 77 Wesleyan schools have been established, providing accommodation for 13,306 scholars. Of these 31 were newly built, at a cost of 22,187/., towards twelve of which the Committee of Council has voted 3,564/. 10s. lOrf. : 46 others have been formed in existing Sunday Schools at a cost, for fitting them up, of 2,883/. f " The schools shall bo of a distinctively religious character; and, as a practical means to realise this purpose, the Bible shall bo daily read and explained, accompanied with devotional singing and prayer; the Wesleyan catechism shall be used, except where parents object; and the children arc required to attend some place of worship on the Lord's Day." "They shall avoid a latitudinarian character, by being avowedly connected with Wesleyan Methodism, while, at the same time, they shall also avoid a sectarian exclusiveness, by admitting children whose parents, of whatever denomination, shall voluntarily place them in these schools."—Minutes of Conference, 1841.

t This, and much other information, has teen kindly supplied by the Rev. M. C. Taylor, Secretaly of the Wesleyan General Education Committee. The constitution of Wesleyan Methodism affords greater facilities than exist in other bodies for the collection of statistics, and those relating to Wesleyan education appear to be remarkably full and accurate.

It is stated by Mr. Taylor that there are several schools (which appear in the Census Tables among *Private* Schools) conducted on Wesleyan trust property, for the use of which no rent is paid, and in support of which, therefore, the Wesleyan body may be said to contribute to the extent of the annual value of such premises. The last Conference resolved to include these Roman CathoLics.

The Roman Catholics stand *fourth* among the denominations in the number of day schools which they more or less support; viz. 339, containing 41,382 scholars. They receive, by virtue of a special minute in their favour, aid from the Parliamentary grant, and have a Government inspector appointed with the sanction of their " Poor School Committee." With them, as well as with the other religious bodies, considerable activity has lately been exhibited, as will appear by reference to the dates at which 311 of their schools, which appear in Class III., were founded:—

Returns respecting income were received from 108 schools containing 14,965 scholars; The total amount for the year 1850 was 10,8922., obtained from the following sources:—*permanent endowment,* 2201.; *voluntary contributions,* 5,1042.; *grants from Government,* 6262.; *payments by scholars,* 4,4952.; *other sources,* 4472. This yields an average annual income of 14s. "id. per scholar.

The Baptists.
Other religious
British Schools.

One hundred and thirty-one schools, containing 9,390 scholars, are reported to be in connexion with the Baptist body.f The Baptists, however, are generally adverse to denominational action in the matter of day school education!; hence the resources of the body are in great degree applied to the support of purely *British* schools. Their teachers were usually trained at the Borough Road Institution until that Society accepted Government aid; since which event they are generally obtained from the training establishment of the "Voluntary School Society." It will, therefore, be apparent that the Baptists are opposed to State-interposition in the work of education.

The provision made by other religious bodies § is comparatively small; the whole together being 331 schools, containing 33,551 scholars.

The preceding enumeration, however, of schools supported by religidus bodies, leaves unmentioned a large class of British schools, which, being maintained by a combination of persons of different communions, and not connected with any particular congregation, have been classified as " *Undenominational."* The The number of places of worship belonging to the Roman Catholics in England and Wales appears, from the Census Report on Religious Worship, to be 570, having accommodation for 186,111 persons. The number of *attendants* on the Census Sunday is estimated at 305,393. The total number of persons of this faith in England and Wales cannot be less than 1,000,000, and probably exceeds this number. From the return as to " birthplace" it appears that as many as 510,959 Of the persons resident in England at the time of the Census were born in Ireland: these would be nearly all Roman Catholics; and to them must be added a further number for the children of such persons born since their settlement in England, and also all the English Roman Catholics.

t The Baptists, according to the Census Returns of Religious Worship, have 2,789 places of worship, with accommodation for 752,343 persons. X " Resolved, That the Union adhere to their declaration in 1844, that' a decided preference is duo to the system of co-operation with the friends of scriptural education at large over that of forming denominational schools,' and altogether repudiate the idea of Sir J. K. Shuttleworth, that public education is the work of the religious communions; an idea which, if practically carried out, would require the impossible result, that every religious communion, however small, should have an establishment of schools spread over the whole country, at least co-extensive with the diffusion of its members."

§ The number of places of worship belonging to all religious bodies, except the five hero named, is stated In the Report on Religious Worship to be 7,208, with accommodation for 1,440,854 worshippers.

number of such schools is seen to be 514 with 82,597 scholars. But to obtain a view of the *total* number of British schools (i. e. schools conducted on the principles of the British and Foreign School Society) there must be a certain number added of the schools which *ate* connected with particular bodies, and which yet retain the distinctive features, and some of them the name, of British schools. The effect of an addition of all such as, though connected with particular bodies, are distinctly styled in the returns *British* schools, will be to raise the number of such schools to 857, and the number of scholars to 123,496. But even this would be an insufficient statement; for no doubt a certain number, not *described* as British schools, are really such—conducted wholly on the British system, and receiving, many of them, teachers from the Normal schools of the British and Foreign School Society. The extent of any further addition to be made on this account can hardly be, with any approach to certainty, computed. Mr. Dunn, the secretary of the society, is stated to estimate the number of scholars in British schools at upwards of 200,000. The difficulty is to lay down any positive definition of a "British" school, since the society does not affiliate any of its local institutions—regarding itself rather as the representative of a *principle* than of persons or classes. The fundamental principles of the society are as follow:—

I. That in all schools established in connexion with or assisted by the British and Foreign School Society, the Holy Scriptures in the authorized version, or extracts therefrom, shall be read and taught daily.

II. That no catechism, or other formulary peculiar to any religious denomination, shall be introduced or taught during the usual hours of school instruction. III. That every child attending the day school shall be expected to attend the particular place of worship or Sunday school which its parents prefer.

Every school, therefore, which conforms to these fundamental principles may be considered to be a British school; and if this definition be adopted, the estimate of Mr. Dunn will rather be exceeded than reduced; for the schools of *Congregationalisis* are wholly of this character; so are those of the *Baptists;* while *Wesleyan* schools, although a catechism is employed, to some extent embody the same principle, since the children are left free to attend the Sunday school or place of worship which their parents may prefer. In the same way, *Ragged Schools,* and subscription schools not associated with any society or denomination, may be classed as "British," since they are supported for the most part by the joint subscriptions of churchmen and dissenters, and are conducted upon non-exclusive principles. The denominational movement of recent years will have the effect, however, of diminishing the *apparent* strength of the British and Foreign School Society; since the various bodies will no doubt be inclined in future to call the schools sustained by their exertions after their own names.

The " British and Foreign School Society" has now been in existence and activity for nearly half a century. During that period above 3,000 teachers have been trained. At the present time its Normal Seminary in the Borough Road has accommodation for sixty resident candidates, and about that number usually attend as out-door pupils. The model schools attached have 1,000 children (700 boys and 300 girls) in daily attendance, and since their establishment upwards of 60,000 have been instructed. There is also a depository of books and school material. Provision is made for inspection of local schools connected with the society. Great improvements have in recent years been made in the methods of tuition, and the most conspicuous advantages of collective teaching have been grafted into the monitorial system.f Public Education, by Sir J. K. Shuttleworth, Bart., p. 142.

The society accepts the co-operation of Government. Of the 133 students now in course of training at its Normal Seminary, 50 are Queen's scholars, receiving yearly exhibitions from the Privy Council. Of the local schools connected with the society, most have, at one time or another, been aided by grants, and are under Government inspection. The income of the society for the year last past was 15,183/. The income, for the year 1850, of 628 British schools (containing 91,944 scholars), has been stated in the Census returns to have been 59,132/., which gives an average per scholar of 12s. *id.* annually. The sources from which this income was derived were—*permanent endowment,* 829/.; *voluntary contributions,* 24,150/.; *grants from Government,* 4,4551.; *payments by scholars,* 26,590/.; *other sources,* 3,108/. The progress of British schools, so far as shown by the dates of establishment

Class IV. The fourth class of schools is designed to represent chiefly such as, deriving

Schools.dbli0 their main support from private subscriptions, are unconnected with religious bodies, or, if connected with them, only incidentally. The following is the list:—

Table 19.

It will be seen from this, that by far the greater proportion of scholars in this class is absorbed by three of the above descriptions of schools; viz., by *ragged schools,* by *factory schools,* and by *schools of no specific character.* These together accommodate nearly 100,000 out of the 109,000 scholars.

The other five British schools are included in Class II., being principally supported by endowment. t There are only nine ragged schools connected with particular denominations: the total of schools is therefore 132, containing 23,643 scholars.

The *Ragged Schools* now form a very important part of our educational pro-*Ragged Schools.* vision; reaching, as they do, those very classes of our population whose repeated criminality and gross obtrusive vice provoke the loud demand now heard for further education, while they hitherto have been untouched, and seem to be almost intangible, by any other agency. It is not easy to assign to any definite period the origin of ragged schools. By some it may be thought that the Sunday school set up by Raikes at Gloucester in 1781, for the outcasts of that city, was essentially a ragged school; but undoubtedly the movement in an organized and vigorous form is the birth of recent years. In 1844 there were only sixteen r&gged schools, having 2,000 children, and 200 (all voluntary) teachers. In that year the " Ragged School Union" was established, and in 1853 there appear to have been in London alone upwards of 116 schools, with 27,676 scholars, and 221 paid and 1,787 voluntary teachers. According to the Census returns, the number of ragged schools in the whole of England and Wales, in 1851, was 132, containing 23,643 scholars. This is an addition to the number in Table 19 of nine schools, which are returned as supported by particular religious bodies, viz., five by the Church of England (containing 800 scholars), three by the Independents (containing 430 scholars), and one by the Baptists (containing 76 scholars). It is not improbable that other ragged schools, inadequately described in the returns, may have been referred to other parts of the classification.

The primary object of the Ragged School is to convert incipient criminals to Christianity: the Bible therefore is in daily use in all, and other means of exerting a religious influence are constantly employed. On Sundays they are, most of them, regular Sunday schools. But it is seen that mere instruction is not likely to be efficacious if the temporal condition of the scholars remain unalleviated and the formidable obstacles to moral influence which utter destitution offers remain unremoved. Accordingly, all ragged schools, in greater or less degree, attempt a double object—both to cultivate the minds and hearts of vagrant children and to raise their physical and social state. In many schools the Scottish plan, of *feeding* the children, is adopted; and in some a limited number are both fed and lodged. In London there are refuges or dormitories, with accommodation for 270 children. The next thing is to fit these children to obtain an honest and industrious livelihood; and with this view much attention is bestowed upon industrial training. Between 40 and 50 schools in London have industrial classes, either daily or on certain evenings, attended by above 2,000 scholars. And the process is pursued yet further; for the children thus instructed are not then abandoned: efforts are put forth to get them suitably employed. With this intention has been founded, under the auspices of the Ragged School Union, the "Shoe-black Society," which gives employment to 37 boys, whose average weekly earnings each were 7s. *id.* in 1853. Some girls have also been employed as "steppers," to sweep and clean door-steps, at *d.* each:—at this they earn about *Ad.* a day. Other children are put into situations:—out of 44 schools, no less than 1,021 children (555 boys and 466 girls) were thus provided for in the year 1852-3; and it is stated that, in some places, children from ragged schools are preferred by employers before those from Union workhouses—so much superior in moral effect is the training they receive from voluntary teachers.f Finally, the best behaved and most industrious scholars are assisted to *emigrate*—as many as 370 having thus been, aided since the formation of the "Ragged School Union." These shoe-blacks are selected from the various schools. They consist of the most meritorious lads of from 13 to 16 years of age. The money received by the boys is paid by them to the society, and appropriated thus:—out of 7s. lid. tho lad gets 4s. *Sd.* for himself at once; Is. *Sd.* goes towards his expenses; and Is. *7d.* is placed to his credit in a savings' bank.—Ninth Annual Report of the Ragged School Union, 1853. Evidence of Mr. William Locke before the Parliamentary Committee (1852) on Criminal and Destitute Juvenile.

The collateral advantages connected with ragged schools are also various and considerable. There are working meetings for the mothers of the children— libraries and reading rooms for the scholars—penny banks for clothing funds f —and similar institutions for encouraging morality and providence.

It would perhaps be difficult too highly to appreciate the value of the Ragged School, and still more difficult to over-estimate the self-denying labours of the nearly 2,000 voluntary teachers by whose Christian fieal alone it is maintained.:): Without the ragged school, the dangerous mass of ignorant depravity would probably continue long impenetrable by moral influence; and it seems to be considered that without the voluntary teachers the moral influence which now the ragged school undoubtedly exerts would not be long preserved.

The Census returns mention the income for 79 Jigged schools containing 15,147 scholars. The total amount is returned at 11,065/.; derived, of course, almost exclusively, from voluntary contributions; being an average of 14s. *Id.* per scholar. This proportion applied to the whole number of scholars (23,643) would give a total income for England and Wales of 17,667/.; but this, it is evident, cannot represent the whole amount contributed and expended for ragged schools; since, where the scholars are fed, the annual expense of each is about *61.;* and where they are both fed and lodged, it is about 8i.§ The income of the Ragged School Union for 1852-3 was about 4,000i. Out of this the Union makes grants to local schools, and provides for regular visitation? The

Union is constructed on an unsectarian basis—its committee being composed of members of the Church of England, Scottish Presbyterians, Independents, Baptists, and Wesleyan Methodists; and this principle of combination is adopted in nearly all the local schools.

Factory Schools. The *Factory Schools* are a consequence of the Acts which regulate the employment of children and young persons in factories. These Acts require that every child between 8 and 13 years of age, employed in any factory, must M#end » school for three hours daily for five days every week. The schoolmaster is to certify that the requisite attendance has been given; and without such certificate the employment of a child is illegal. But the schools may either be within the factories—established by the owners specially for the children they employ—or they may be private or denominational schools outside. It appears, from information furnished by Mr. Horner and Mr. Redgrave, that the number of children in schools *inside* of factories is between 6,000 and 7,000. Hence it follows that rather more than 10,000 of the above number (17,835) were in schools outside the factories—established, probably, with a special view to factory children, and thus called "Factory Schools." As the total number of children between eight and thirteen occupied in factories in England and Wales in 1850 was stated at 34,155, the difference between the 17,834 and this 34,155 (vifi. 16,321) must be the number of factory 1children who attend denominational or other similar schools.

The inspectors of factories point out that many of the schools in which these children pass the stated number of hours are far from being of a satisfactory „,« n London *M* schools have libraries: some with onlv 40 or B0 volumes, but some with 300 or 400, and one with 800.—Ninth Report of the Ragged School Union.

T Into these, parents or children may, once a week or so, drop Id., *id.,* or even *id.* This, accumulating tor six or twelve months, is then increased by the liberality of friends, and expended in suitable clothing, or the materials for it; and by this means it is found that in twelve months a school is so changed and improved that it is not like the same place, nor the children like the same beings. In a return from 42 schools, no less than 529. has been thus received and expended during the year."—Ninth Report.

t The ordeal through which a Ragged School teacher has to pass is occasionally one of no trilling character. Mr. Locke describes himself as having been sometimes obliged, by the attacks of his *pnUgia, to*flj Jam the school and seek the protection of the police. *I* £TMtencc of Mr. Win. Lockj before tho Committee on Criminal and Destitute Juveniles. II Parliamentary Return No. 745. character. The inspectors indeed have power to annul certificates; but so long as the schoolmaster can write and the school is supplied with materials for teaching it seems that no such course can be adopted. There is therefore no security, beyond the fact that inefficient schools are generally now becoming scarcer, that the time appropriated to the children's school attendance shall be usefully employed. On the other hand, there is evidence that, in spite of these defects, the law has produced considerable benefit to this class of children; and it seems to be considered that the necessary *regularity* of their attendance, though for only three hours daily, gives them an advantage very much compensating the greater opportunities in other ways possessed by other scholars.f

The large number (717) of schools which are stated to be *of no specific Schools of m character* is made up chiefly by such as are inadequately described in the JJJJ1"" returns; the only fact by which they could be classified at all being that of their support by voluntary contributions. Probably, therefore, some of them belong to religious bodies, and some perhaps are British schools.

The only other description of schools included in this class which seems to require remark is the *industrial school.* Of this description there are stated to be six schools—the meaning being that that number are returned as "Industrial Schools," without any further definition. Of course there are many more schools in which industrial occupations are pursued; and probably these six might, if a fuller description had been given, have been classified in another manner.

2. Evening Schools Fob Children.

Evening schools for children were, for various reasons—principally on account of practical difficulties in the way of any satisfactory enumeration of them—not included in the Educational Census. There can be no doubt, however, that they form a very important part of educational provision, and their number must be far from inconsiderable. But compared with their importance, little has yet been done in this department. When it is considered that the principal obstacle to the continuous education of the working classes is the great demand for early labour, causing constant occupation through the daytime, it would seem that evening schools presented just the remedy required. It is indeed objected that the previous toil is likely to unfit the child for study; but a well-conducted school might easily make study so attractive as to be in truth a recreation.

" The millowner cannot legally employ a child without having obtained certificates of its having attended school; and the parent is responsible if it be permitted to neglect school; but the law has imposed no condition and provided no security that anything shall nave been learnt at school. The master must be able to teach, and have the materials for teaching, reading, and writing; but of the occupation of time in school, and of its results, the law takes no cognifiance." —Report of Alexander Redgrave, Esq., for the half year ended 31st October 1852. Sep also the Evidence of Leonard Horner, Esq., before the Parliamentary Committee on the Manchester and Salford Education Bill, Session 1853. t See Letter of Rev. W. J. Kennedy to Leonard Horner, Esq. Report for half year ended 30th April 1863. SECONDARY EDUCATION.

The assertion may perhaps be safely made that more than half the time and labour spent on primary instruction in the elementary day-school will be spent in vain unless the educational process there commenced shall be continued afterwards. In fact, by far the greater portion of the usual school-time, more especially of the working classes, is devoted to the acquisition of mere instruments for gaining knowledge—not to the acquisition of knowledge itself. If, therefore, no facilities be offered for the future *application* of these instruments—if, reading and writing having been acquired, no opportunities present themselves for putting into useful exercise these means of information—it can scarcely be a matter of surprise that multitudes, in spite of an accessible supply of elementary schools, should still remain uneducated. The immense importance, then, of *secondary* education, cannot but be recognised. Indeed, it *has* been recognised, and various plans, some very extensive, in imitation of the Continental systems, have been advocated. Nor has the Government been wholly inactive in this direction, having recently established the "Department of Practical Science and Art" for the purpose of encouraging a higher education in those arts and sciences the cultivation of which is absolutely necessary to secure industrial excellence.f

The information gathered at the Census as to the extent and character of secondary education then existing is, I fear, but scanty. Time will suffer me to do no more than merely indicate the prominent results of what *has* been collected. This relates to two descriptions of establishments; vifi., *Evening Schools for Adults,* and *Literary, Scientific, and Mechanics' Institutions.* 1. Evening Schools For Adults.

The number of Evening Schools from which returns were obtained was 1545; containing 39,783 students, of whom 27,829 were males and 11,954 were females. The amount of payment weekly varied from *Id.* to *2s.*: the actual number of schools at each of several rates of charge being thus —

Charge. No. of Schools.
Free....-2
Less than *2d.* per week... 231
2d. and less than *3d.*-122
3d. ,, 4d. ..---333
4d. ,, bd. ---106
bd. and upwards.... 294
Payment not stated-.-457

Some of the schools were open every evening, while others were confined to a certain number of nights per week. So, some were open all the year round, See, amongst several, "A Lecture delivered at the Mechanics Institution, Manchester, Nov. 14, 1853," by Rev. 0. Richson, M.A.

t Beturns respecting art education were not obtained at the Census. From a table published by the above-mentioned department, it appears that there were, in 1851, twelve schools of design in England and Wales; vifi., at Birmingham, Coventry, Leeds, Manchester, Newcastle, Norwich, Nottingham, Potteries, Sheffield, Spitalflelds, York, and the London Central School; the average attendance of students during the year being 2,287. The fees were generally about 2s. per month. Since the formation (in February 1852) of the Department of Practical Art, under the superintendence of H. Cole, C.B., and R. Redgrave, Esq., the whole system of these schools of design has been completely reformed. Encouragement to local schools is given by this department in six ways — 1. A well-organified system of inspection and direction; 2. A supply of good examples, models, apparatus, books, and other articles, at moderato prices; 8. A supply of properly educated masters; 4. The admission of the students of local schools to peculiar privileges at the central institution at Marlborough House, cither by allowing them access to its collections, books, or lectures, on favourable terms, or by electing them to scholarships and exhibitions, with a view to their studying at it; 5. The delivering of lectures by competent persons at the local schools; 6. Pecuniary assistance, chiefly in the form of guarantees of masters' salaries. (See Imports of Committees of Inquiry into Public Offices.) One prominent feature of the policy of the department is its tendency to create *self-supporting* schools: indeed, it is anticipated that the central school itself may bo expected to be shortly independent of the aid of Government. while others were closed for a certain number of months. The facts upon these points will he found in Table S., *post,* pp. 144-145.

The following Table shows the *occupations* of the scholars who availed themselves of these facilities:—

Table 21. will show, in some degree, the course of instruction pursued in these evening schools. Some of these are very superior and capable of producing very important benefits.

As an illustration, the National school of St. Thomas, Charterhouse, may be mentioned. The "advanced classes" there are instructed by competent masters in the Latin, French, and Gormau languages, in history, geography, book-keeping, and various other studies, for 5s. and upwards per quarter, The Rev, Wm. Rogers, M.A, the incumbent, himself conducts two of the classes.

E

The distribution of these schools over the country may be seen by reference to Table S. *(post,* Summary Tables, pp. 144-145.) 5 from which it appears that Lancashire and the West Riding of Yorkshire stand at the head of the List of Counties— greatly exceeding all the others. The neglected state of London will be obvious on considering that Middlesex contained but 76 schools with only 1,733 scholars. But, no doubt, the returns as to evening schools were defective.

2. Literary, Scientific, And Mechanics' Institutions.

Intelligence was received respecting 1,057 of these institutions; several, however, being scarcely of the character conveyed by the above title. Some were merely " Mutual Improvement Societies," established in connection with Sunday schools, while others partook more of the nature of professional institutions, for the benefit of the members of particular professions. Time would not permit the attempt to classify them. These are *Registration* Counties, consisting of aggregates of entire Districts or Unions.

T The large number of these valuable

institutions in Yorkshire is, no doubt, in a great degree, to be ascribed to the operations of the " Yorkshire Union of Mechanics' Institutes,'' of which Mr. Edward Baines, its founder, is the President. This union, by its meetings, reports, lecturw, itinerating village libraries, and other operations for increasing the number and improving the management of these institutions, has, during the seventeen years of its existence, been extremely useful. The number of institutions associated in this voluntary union, in 1853, was 127, with an aggregate of between 19,000 and 20,000 members.

SUNDAY SCHOOLS

There were, at the time of the Census, 23,514 Sunday Schools in England and Wales, having enrolled upon their hooks 2,407,642 scholars, taught by 318,135 teachers. On the Census Sunday, 1,817,499 at leastf of these scholars actually attended at their schools.

These figures, of themselves, must necessarily produce in many minds a feeling of surprise at the vast extent of an educational machinery which, whatsoever its efficiency, has nearly covered the whole surface of the country and embraced all classes of inhabitants. No adequate idea, it is evident, can be obtained of England's real educational condition unless some opinion first be formed concerning the position which the Sunday school should occupy amongst the various institutions now in operation for instructing and improving the community.

The opinions actually expressed, by public writers, of the value of the Sunday school, considerably vary: some appear to estimate its influence but lightly, others look upon it as of vast importance. This divergence probably is mainly owing to the different points of view from which the institution is regarded—some considering only its facilities for giving secular instruction, while the others rather judge it as a means of religious training.

Little hesitation need be felt in describing the Sunday school as a *religious* institution. This, indeed, it has been from its very commencement; for, whatever may have been the primary vague design of its benevolent originator, certain is it that the spirit which impelled the movement forward so triumphantly, and which so vigorously still ensures its progress, was and is the offspring of religious zeal. It is not for the sake of imparting secular instruction that 318,000 members of the various churches voluntarily every week assume the teacher's office; but for the purpose of inculcating religious truth, and exerting a religious influence. If children in the Sunday school are taught to read, it is only for the purpose of removing an impediment to the grand design: the primer and the letter-box are doubtless looked upon as merely temporary instruments, to be resigned with gladness when the art of reading shall be universally acquired elsewhere. Far, therefore, from conceiving that the spread of daily education is to cause the disappearance of the Sunday school, as having done its work, its friends anticipate with hope a period of secular enlightenment, in which, relieved from all mere introductory labour, they may give their undivided energies to their especial object.

Probably the true position of the Sunday school will be more accurately estimated after a brief description of a few of its peculiar features, which may not perhaps be known to all.

In general, every local Sunday school is the offshoot of an individual congregation, from the midst of which the teachers are selected. It is managed by a committee, having for its president the Minister. Its officers are a secretary, treasurer, and superintendent, generally chosen annually by the teachers. The The Sabbath School and Bible Teaching; by James Inglis.—Sundny School Teaching practically considered; by the R'v. F. J. Serjeant.-The Sunday School;;i Prize Essay; by Louisa Davids.—directions for the Establishment and Mfmcgemont of Sunday Schools; by the Sunday School Union. —Collins's Teachers' Companion.— The distinctive Features of the Sunday School; a Lecture; by J. G. Fleet.—Our Sunday Schools: what they do;tnd what they might do for England; by Edward Baines.—Senior Classes, and the Mode of conducting thein; by W. H. Watson. —The Senior Class; a Prize Essay by J. A. Cooper.—The Infant Class in the Sunday School; a Prize Essay; by Charles Reed.—History of the Sunday School Union; by W. H. Watson.

+ This number attended *at one time;* i. e. only the number present at one particular portion of the day was returned. In some schools this portion would be the morning; but generally it would be the afternoon. Those scholars, therefore, who attended only during the portion of the day for which the return was *not* made are not included in this number; and for these a considerable addition should be made in order to obtain the total number who attended at any part of the Census Sunday. scholars, who, though mainly, are not exclusively composed of the working class, are mostly upwards of six years of age; but the tendency is now to establish infant classes for all between three and six. The proportion of *adults* in Sunday schools considerably varies in different districts of the country; Wales and the manufacturing counties having very many upwards of 14 years, while London has but very fewf. Unfortunately, no inquiry was made at the Census as to the *age* of Sunday scholars, so that we are still without complete intelligence on this important point. This difference of age in the scholars necessarily involves the distribution of them into different classes, suited to their varying attainments: there is the *infant* class, as above referred to, for the children under six— the *ordinary* class for children between six and fourteen (divided into two or three sections, according to their ability to read)—and the *senior* class for young persons upwards of 14. Registers are kept, in which the names and addresses of the scholars are inserted—their admission and departure chronicled—and their attendances from Sunday to Sunday noted.

There are usually two school-attendances each Sunday, one in the morning, beginning about nine or half-past nine o'clock, and the other in the afternoon, commencing about two. On each occasion school is opened with devotional exercises—such as singing, reading of the Scriptures, and prayer. Next, the scholars who have committed tasks to memory repeat them. Then, the Bible lesson follows: portions of Scripture having been allotted to particular Sundays, scholars are expected to come prepared, by week-day study of the passage, for a catechetical examination by the teacher, who on his part ought to come prepared by similar study, to impart the full meaning of the text, and to enforce its doctrines. To enable teachers to discharge this duty worthily, it is now the practice for the several "Unions %" which have been established for the guidance and improvement of the system, to supply an exposition of each lesson in the form of ample "Notes," by which the teachers are assisted to a right conception of the passage, and a proper application of its truth. This is the course pursued with scholars who can read: to infants and to others who have not yet learnt the art, more elementary instruction must be given. This, however, is only given with a view to scripture-reading, and the method usually adopted is—from a box of moveable letters to construct a scripture verse, which thus becomes impressed upon the children's minds and is then explained to them familiarly by the teacher. In the *senior* class the same plan is pursued as in the ordinary classes of children able to read; except that, of course, a superior ability of teaching is required. Indeed, an efficient instructor of a senior class has need, apparently, of information and capacity but little inferior to what is necessary for the regular ministry. § The school concludes, as it commenced, with singing and prayer.—preceded generally, in the afternoon, by a short address from the minister or some other person competent to the task.

Soo the Infant Class in the Sunday School; a Prifie Essay; hy Charles Reed. It is estimated that the number of Sunday scholars under six years of age is about a sixth of the whole. t It appears. from returns supplied to the Church of England Sunday School Institute, that in London the proportion of scholars above fifteen is only four per cent.; while, in the manufacturing districts it is as high as twenty-five per cent. (Lecture on the distinctive Features of the Sunday School; by J. G. Fleet, Esq.) The writer of this lecture estimates the proportion in *Enqlani)*, above fifteen, at *a tenth* of the whole. Another writer states that in a Sunday school in Manchester the average age of the individuals composing the elder class of females was found to be Wi years, and in the elder class of males $17i$ years. Also that in a school at Halifax, containing 500 scholars, 160 wero more than sixteen years of age; and that one of the three classes connected with another school contained fifty-seven females whose ages varied from sixteen to forty-five. (W. H.Watson on Senior Classes, page 7.) Similar facts arc mentioned in Mrs. David's Essav on the Sunday School, p. 160. Mr. Reed estimates the number at an *eighth* or a *ninth.* 1 The Church of England schools are assisted in this way by the " Church of England Sunday School Institute," formed in 1844. The Wesleyan schools are under the management of the Educational Committee appointed by_ Conference. The " Sunday School Union," formed upon an unsectarian basis, was established in 1803, and renders aid to most of the Dissenters' Sunday schools. It was by this union that the plan was first originated. § See Watson's " Senior Classes:" Inglis's "Sabbath School:" Cooper's Prifie Essay on the Sunday School Senior Class,

From this it will be evident how vast an influence must necessarily be exercised by Sunday-school instruction on the minds of the English people. The simple fact alone that 318,000 persons, mostly young, are thus obliged, in order to discharge their voluntary functions, to acquire, by careful study, an intelligent acquaintance with the Scriptures, is of no slight value. Doubtless much of the instruction given is comparatively ineffective—many teachers being found inadequate to their position, and the methods of instruction being often injudicious. But advancement is continually being made: the various improvements introduced in day school teaching have been carried into Sunday schools, and the unremitting vigor and sagacity of those who, at the central "Unions," watch for every opportunity of further progress, cannot fail to raise up shortly an efficient band of teachers well adapted for the more advanced intelligence of future generations. Even now, perhaps, the actual results of Sunday school instruction are but ill-appreciated. We perceive, indeed, the great improvement which has taken place within the past half century in the manners of the people—their increased attachment to the cause of order and sobriety; and the contrast of our land, in this respect, with other countries, often furnishes the theme for gratulation; but the share which Sunday schools have taken in effecting this desirable result is probably to a great extent unrecognized. And yet the constant action on the minds of the youthful population, of more than a quarter of a million of religious teachers—not removed in general by age or sex from sympathy with their companions—each, too, having such a limited number of scholars as to make the influence direct and personal— must needs be working silently a great result. Intelligent familiarity with scriptural facts and doctrines must be gradually extending through the masses of society; and though, if tested merely by attendance on religious ordinances, much of this instruction may appear to be in vain, yet, doubtless, in a thousand other ways, though imperceptible, the influence exerted in the Sunday school is more or less prolonged throughout the subsequent career and mainly helps to bring about that increase of morality and deference to law on which, from time to time, our public writers dwell with much complacency. Indeed, it may be very fairly questioned whether Sunday-school instructors do not exercise an influence, in moulding the religious mind of the community, considerably more extensive and more potent than proceeds from all the pulpits in the land.

But this extensive influence does not result exclusively from the mere instruction which is given. The position and the character of the teachers members of the middle class; the evident disinterestedness of their gratuitous exertions; the personal attachment which not seldom binds a teacher to his pupils f, and the friendly interest with which he often aids them in their secular career; all these and many more *collateral* advantages of Sunday schools combine to give the system its extensive and benignant power. Much more, it is true, might be accomplisheu in this way than is effected; for the *capabilities* of Sunday schools, in this respect, are almost boundless; but the actual and prejent efforts are of striking value. Visits from the teachers to the scholars Amongst the means employed and suggested for this purpose are preparation-classes of the teachers. The plan is, to meet on a week-evening with the minister, and go over the lesson fixed for the ensuing Sunday. Where the minister does not do this (too often the case), the superintendent or some suitable person is chosen to preside. A scheme is also being tried of giving, in a meeting of teachers, *model lessons.*—Sunday School Teaching practically considered; oy the liev. P. Or. Serjeant, p. 101. Another plan is conducted more upon the *mutual* principle: each member of the class undertaking some particular portion of the lesson, and all deriving the advantage of each other's labours. In London the teachers of all schools in connection with the Sunday School Union have access, at a trifling charge, to a large theological library.

t A striking instance is related of a teacher who was obliged suddenly to seek surgical assistance in one of the metropolitan hospitals. "When the young people came to the place of instruction, and found their teacher gone, they learnt where he was, and proceeded thither with their Bibles: and every Sunday, while he continued there, these youths formed a class round his bed, and received, to the astonishment of the other patients in the ward, the scriptural instruction of their much-loved teacher. "—Senior Classes, by W. H. Watson. in their homes are frequent; and not rare are visits from the scholars to the teachers. Many schools sustain week-evening classes, where the scholars are instructed in some secular art or knowledge: many have libraries for the scholars' use; and some have originated, for the senior scholars, "Mutual Improvement Societies," where lectures are delivered, and other means of intellectual progress are provided. Nor are the physical wants of Sunday scholars and their parents without some alleviation. Sick cluhs, and provident clubs, and penny banks are frequently established in connexion with the Sunday school. Excursions, too, and festivals, in which the children and their teachers join in recreation, are now universal. Thus there is, in some degree (although too small), a constant kindly intercourse between the different classes of society; and thus, perhaps, are being gradually fostered in the minds of the working people juster sentiments than hitherto have been received of the disposition of the class by fortune placed above them. But in this department of its usefulnesss the Sunday school is yet but in its infancy; awaiting, probably, the time when ministers and influential members of the Church shall recognize its undeveloped power for good. *Their* zealous aid appears to be the only thing required in order that the great advantages, direct and incidental, of the system, may be fully realized— the youthful population get a sound religious education—and the sad estrangement, now too visible, between the different sections of society, be gradually healed. It is, doubtless, much to be desired that more attention should be paid by the higher classes of the Church to the working of what now has every appearance of a permanent institution; for no expectation, probably, can be indulged that the natural instructors of their children in religious knowledge (viz. parents) will be ever generally able and disposed to undertake and prosecute this duty; and it seems to be quite clear that the ordinary services of church and chapel are entirely inappropriate and unproductive to the juvenile community.f Both, therefore, as a necessary and effective institution for the spiritual culture of the young, and as a most important means of binding up in harmony the various orders of the people, Sunday schools appear to their supporters to be worthy of the countenance and active aid of the highest intelligence of the Christian Church.%

Efforts are now being made to extend the Sunday school in two directions— i downwards and upwards; to admit the scholars at an earlier age, and retain them till a later. The *infant class* is designed for children between three and six, who have not been hitherto admitted generally. The *senior class* is intended, for young persons, who, arriving at the age of 14 or 15, have outgrown the ordinary course of Sunday-school tuition. The former is conceived to be essential to a perfect scheme of Sunday schools, in order that the child may be prepared, by proper training at the most impressible age, for subsequent instruction in the ordinary school; the latter is of obvious necessity, in order that the good effect produced in the ordinary school may be preserved and strengthened. Both of these schools are distinct from the main school, being held in different apartments or localities. h

The composition of the *infant class* is of course very different from that of the ordinary class. Instead of only eight or ten pupils to a teacher, the number varies from 60 to 150, who are usually taught by the collective method These libraries are 'in great measure supplied by the Sunday School Union, which, indeed, prepares a great many of the works, and selects or approves the whole. When it is considered that these books aro omen read by the *families* of the scholars, it will be clear that much is being done in this way to counteract the influence of that unwholesome literature which is unfortunately the cheapest.

t So evident is this, that the plan is now to a considerable extent adopted of having *separate services* for children, conducted by experienced teachers.—See the arguments for and against this plan in tho Church of England Sunday School Teacher's Quarterly Magazine,

December 1853. *t* The Sabbath Schooland Bible Teaching; by Jas. Inglis,pp,llS,H9.—Sunday School Teaching practically considered; by the Rev. F. J. Serjeant, p. 106. in a gallery. The Bible-lesson is set up with moveable letters in the lid of the letter-box— the most striking parts of Scripture being chosen; and this is dwelt upon *pictorially* by the teacher, and its doctrine familiarly illustrated and applied. The number of scholars under six years of age has been computed at about 400,000. The total number of children, of all ranks, between three and six, in England and Wales, may be stated at 1,338,890; and of those between three and *seven* at 1,765,420. The proportion of these belonging to the working classes would be about 1,004,168 and 1,324,065 respectively.

But the *senior class* is the grand *desideratum* to the perfect working of the Sunday-school system, for without some means of continuing instruction and maintaining influence when the scholar enters the most critical period of life the chances are that what has been already done will prove to have been done in vain. This is, indeed, made manifest by the returns of religious worship; for, unquestionably, most of the four or five millions who are constantly away from public worship must have passed through the Sunday school. It is, therefore, proposed to establish, in every school, a higher class for young persons upwards of 14; the course of instruction in which shall be of a more elaborate character than that of the general school. It is thought that, by throwing an air of dignity around the senior class, many may be attracted to attend it who would feel unwilling to be mingled with the children in the general school. But in proportion to the importance of these senior classes is the difficulty of establishing and conducting them; a higher order of teachers being needful, whose superiority of intellect and information shall command the willing deference of the scholars, while their hearty sympathy with those they teach shall render the connexion rather one of friendship than of charity. Such classes, too, will not'be 'long continued with efficiency unless the teacher feel so strong an interest in his pupils as to make their secular prosperity a portion of his care. It is obvious, therefore, that the scheme requires for its complete development more aid from those who are in age, position, and intelligence considerably superior to most of the present teachers, and who hitherto have very sparingly contributed their personal efforts to the cause of the Sunday school. The friends, however, of the movement seem to have every confidence that 'the inappreciable value of the plan, as a means of communicating to the people a religious influence which in no other way could reach them, and as tending to unite the two great classes of society, will soon secure the requisite assistance from the fittest members of the Church, f

These are the most conspicuous features of the Sunday school as at present constituted; and perhaps but few can help regarding it as, even in its present state, a most invaluable agent for promoting the religious education of the people and securing social peace, while its capabilities of future and almost indefinite improvement cannot be unrecognized by any. Nor is it possible, perhaps, for any one who, unacquainted with the system and the aims of its promoters, makes it his business to inquire concerning both, to avoid the conviction, that while the labours of above 318,000 voluntary teachers evidence a zeal beyond the reach of commendation, the designs and measures cherished and adopted by the active leaders of the movement are distinguished by an amount of practical skill and wisdom which can scarcely fail to bring about a wide success.

The Infant Class in the Sunday School i by Charles Reed. t The extent to which these classes have actually been formed is at present very limited. Amongst the Wesleyan Methodists they are called " Select Classes:" and the last returns of that body showed only 21,617 in such classes. The Wesleyan Sunday-school arrangements, however, comprise "Catechumen classes" for young persons upwards of twelve years of age, who are placed under the care of lay catechists who meet them weekly, while the minister gives his assistance once a quarter.

The amount of Sunday-school instruction to a given population varies considerably in different portions of the country. As a general rule, perhaps, it may be said that Sunday scholars are most numerous in localities where opportunities for day school education are most wanting. Thus, it will be found that in Wales and in the manufacturing counties of Lancashire and Yorkshire Sunday scholars are very numerous; while in Sussex, Kent, and other counties they are considerably fewer. But the exceptions to this rule are many; and various other circumstances will be found to operate in causing a greater or a less attendance. One of these may be the prevalence, or otherwise, in any district, of dissent; dissenters generally throwing into Sunday schools the energy which churchmen put forth in the more expensive task of raising and sustaining day schools. The following Table (23.) shows the proportion per cent. of Sunday scholars to population in each English county— in North and South Wales—and in several of the larger towns.

If we inquire by what religious bodies in particular these Sunday schools are carried on, we shall find that the Church of England, which possesses more than four-fifths of the day schools, has considerably less than half of the Sunday schools: in fact it is only in comparatively recent years that the Sunday school has found much favour with the Church of England generally—many clergymen apparently possessing conscientious scruples as to the employment of lay agency for religious teaching. The following Table (24.) exhibits the number of Sunday schools and scholars in connexion with each denomination.

One of the principal features of the Sunday school system is the number of *teachers*. Out of the 23,137 schools which made returns, the number of teachers was given for 21,724 containing 2,281,344 scholars. If this proportion be applied to the whole number of scholars the aggregate number of teachers would be 318,135. This gives a proportion of 7'6 scholars to one teacher j but this must be taken subject to the observation that in some parts of the country (more especially in the north of England) a custom prevails of *alternate teaching,* i. e. one set of teachers will attend the morning classes and another set the afternoon, or two sets teach on alternate months.f This practice, however, is generally now discountenanced and is gradually falling into desuetude. On the other hand, in the Infant classes, as many as a hundred scholars will have only one teacher. The proportion of teachers to scholars varies in the different denominations; thus, in the Church of England schools there are 12-3 scholars on an average to a teacher; while the average amongst Independents is 7'8—amongst Baptists 6-4—amongst Wesleyan Methodists 5-2. There is also a variation in particular parts of the country: In this table no estimate has been made for the 377 Sunday schools which sent no returns. 3ee page 10.) thus, while the average of scholars to a teacher is about seven or eight in the whole of England and Wales, in Dorset, Oxford, Surrey, Suffolk, it approches 10,—in Essex, Middlesex, Somerset, Rutland, Sussex, it is close upon 11,—and in Hereford it is just 13. On the other hand, in Cornwall it is less than five—in Yorkshire between five and six—and in Lincolnshire between six and seven.

Out of 301,447 teachers, 10,383 are returned as being paid—vifi. 5,311 males and 5,072 females (See Table Q. p. '.) These are chiefly in Church of England schools; which indeed contain 9,286 out of-the 10,383. No doubt, they are mostly the masters or mistresses of national schools. It is worthy of remark that, on the first establishment of Sunday schools, a salaried staff of teachers was contemplated; it was more by accident than by design that the voluntary plan of tuition, which is now the most valuable portion of the system, was introduced.

The *progress* of Sunday schools in recent years may be roughly gathered from the following Table (25.) showing the *dates* at which existing schools were established; but as, in all probability, the dates returned apply, in some cases, to the period when the *building* was erected, though the school may not have been commenced till afterwards—while, in other cases, schools may have been removed from one locality to another, and the date of the last removal only mentioned; for these and various other reasons the statement must be looked upon with caution. And, of course, it must be recollected that it does not pretend.to give the number of schools existing at each period, but merely the number of now existing schools which were at each period commenced....

The idea of conducting such Institutions by unpaid teachers is said to have originated in a meeting of fiealous Wesleyan office-bearers; one of whom, when the others were lamenting that they had no funds for hiring teachers, said " Let's do it ourselves."

Information as to the place in which instruction was carried on was given for 22,704 schools out of 23,137i The result of this is as follows:—

Church of Dissenters'
Schools held in England Schools. Schools. Total.
Separate buildings-7,087-3,660-10,747
Church or chapel-1,811-7,731-9,542
Part of a house--1,261-1,154. 2,415

The question recurs—How is the standard to be reached?

This review of our existing educational agencies will probably be useful in considering the question now recurring: By what means is the task to be accomplished of attaining the position previously hinted at as being both a satisfactory and practicable standard? How are the various improvements in Dayschool teaching to be carried out? how are the new or altered buildings to be provided? and how are the additional schools, when once established, to be properly sustained? This is the great inquiry which in recent years has occupied, and apparently perplexed, the minds of all who feel concern for the condition of our growing population, and who think and work for its advancement.

Two great parties; one favourable and vention of the State.

It has been already mentioned that a change in the aspect of this great question has occurred within the last few years. Formerly, opinions were totheiiter5Ver8e amos unanimous, that the provision of a large proportion of the necessary funds for popular education was a duty appertaining to the State, *i. e.,* to society at large acting through its representative agents, by the medium of general taxation; the only point of controversy having reference to the mode in which this duty should be exercised in order to secure an adequate protection for the rights of conscience in the matter of *religious* teaching. But, of late years, rather a noticeable change has seriously interrupted this agreement. Whether convinced, by the nature of the legislation actually attempted, of the impossibility of any equitable treatment, by the State, of all religious bodies—or deriving, from the progress of opinion on the free trade question, an enlarged idea of the hurtfulness of Government assistance generally—or impressed, by many evidences, with a sense of the enormous power of individual enterprise and charity when left to their own resources—it is certain that a very considerable number of the earnest friends of education gradually came to the conclusion that the increase and improvement of our popular day schools would be best promoted without any intervention by the State. The country, therefore, may be said to be divided, on the question of *educational agency,* into two great parties—one invoking, and the other deprecating, the employment of the public taxes for the furtherance of education.

Position taken up by the VOlUN' lAEY PAETT.

The position which the Voluntary Party has at length arrived at seems to be as follows:—in the first place, they contend that the provision of instruction for the people does not fall within the legitimate province of the State: in the next place, they assert that any such interference cannot but produce unfortunate results: and, finally, they maintain that the people are well able to provide good education for themselves, and that they are actually doing so as fast as can be reasonably wished.

1. The course of argument by which they think that their first proposition is maintained is principally this:—that any interference of the central power in the matter of education can proceed on no other principle than that it is the right of such central power to *train the mind of the people:* that this principle, if once admitted, necessarily involves the right of the Government to pursue whatever course appears to it best adapted for this end: that the Government would therefore have the right to apply the public funds to the maintenance of newspapers, the provision of theatrical amusements, and to many similar objects, all of which would be considered universally to lie beyond its proper sphere. The duty of providing children's education, they contend, belongs, in the first place, to the *parents;* and there are only two classes of children with regard to whom the State may be considered as *in loco parentis,* viz., prisoners and paupers. 'With respect to these, it is allowed, the State which feeds them bodily must also furnish intellectual nourishment; but all the rest should be provided with instruction by their natural parents, with such aid (if they should be unable to afford the whole expense) as private Christian charity or individual philanthropy may offer. For the *State* to relieve the people of their educational responsibilities would be, it is affirmed, a recognition of the principle of *communism,* just as much as if the children were supplied with daily food or clothing. Many of the voluntary party also, holding that it is impossible, consistently with proper *education,* to exclude religion from the day school, and protesting, as Dissenters, against the application of public money to religious teaching, hence derive another argument against a State interposition. 2. But not only is a State provision for the education of the people inconsistent, in the judgment of the voluntary party, with correct ideas of the province of the delegated Government; it would inevitably, they conceive, if sanctioned, lead to lamentable consequences. Foremost of these they place the injury which would, they think, result to the national character, if thus its most conspicuous virtue, of a sturdy, individual self-reliance, should be undermined, and a habit fostered of transferring individual, and especially parental, duties to the shoulders of the State.f Nor less, it is conceived, to the character of those who now, in aiding of their own free will in the work of popular instruction, find so much to draw forth the highest virtues, would the substitution of compulsion for benevolence prove other than disastrous, tending to extinguish much of that devotion for a worthy object which can only spring from the sense of purely *moral* obligation. For the voluntary party seem to have no faith whatever in the theory that voluntary fieal can be *encouraged* by State bounties: rather, they anticipate, the State having once begun must needs continue and augment its efforts till it finally sustain the burden altogether. This inevitable end attained, instruction will, it is suggested, gradually but certainly grow inefficient: free from the stimulus of competition, the machinery provided at such cost will rust—inspectors, now so active and inventive, will sink down into conservative' routine—and the whole elaborate and expensive system will be just as unimprovable and stagnant as is any other ancient Government department when contrasted with the vigour and progressiveness of private enterprise. 3. But the voluntary party not only say that State interposition is both wrong in principle and certain to prove ineffectual in practice: they maintain that voluntary agency is amply adequate to satisfy our utmost need, both as to quantity and quality of education. In support of this assertion they refer to the many vast achievements, in our day, of individual benevolence and fieal; to the 2,000 buildings raised in twenty years by the voluntary efforts of the Church of England; to the many thousands more, erected by the uncompelled exertions of the various other bodies; to the cost at which all these and all their ministers are annually and willingly supported; to the multitude The following passage (adopted by the Voluntary Party) from one of Dr. Wordsworth's Sermons, will explain their views upon this point:—" Take away from parents among the poor the inducement to make sacrifices for the education of their children,—tempt them by an indiscriminate offer of eleemosynary education to disburden themselves of their children as an irksome and oppressive weight, and to cast them for instruction on a school rate, and transfer them to public tutelage,—let the nation, by a general act of adoption, alienate the children of the poor from their parents, and appropriate them to itself,—let the State be an universal stepmother, what would be the consequence? Children would be no longer regarded by a parent as a blessing for which he ought gladly to spend and be spent, in order that, by his own sacrifices for their education, they might be his crown of rejoicing at the great day. No; the nation would have proclaimed by public enactment that children are a burden from which the poor may reasonably desire to be discharged. Because some among the poor are in a very miserable condition, wo ought not to adopt a system which would tend to demoralifie them all. We ought not to injuro the good and provident among the poor for the sake of the bad; and no condition of things can justify an outrage upon natural instincts, and a dissolution of domestic ties. Nothing can compensate for an infraction of parental rights, and an abrogation of filial duties. Nothing can authorifie a war against the sanctity of home."—Occasional Sermons, No. 22, p.126. t See "Letters to Lord John llussell," by Edward Baines, 1846; " Crosby Hall Lectures on Education;" " Education best promoted by perfect Freedom,—not by State Endowments," by of charitable institutions, hospitals, asylums, colleges; to the long array of religious societies for home arid foreign operations, having more than a million sterling, probably, of ag-

gregate annual income. Impressed by the grandeur of this wonderful display of England's voluntary power, they cannot be persuaded that the agency by which all this has been effected is incompetent to furnish the *assistance* requisite ifl order that the people may be universally and thoroughly instructed. For it must not be Unnoticed that, in estimating the resources of the voluntary principle, its advocates do not restrict their view to the charitable contributions of religious persons or communities: *whatever* influences, other than the force of legal obligation, may be made available to raise, sustain, and improve our educational institutions, are regarded as a portion of the wealth of voluntaryism. Hence, one-great reliance of the party is upon the rich and hitherto but half-developed energies of the people—of the working class—themselves; and it is confidently held that, by encouraging their selfreliance and by stimulating their convictions of parental duty, they may soon be made the principal instead of the subordinate contributors towards their children's education. But not alone from its conspicuous achievements in the various departments named above is the voluntary principle considered by its friends sufficient for our educational emergencies: they think the same conclusion must be reached by viewing its successes hitherto in the very work of popular enlightenment itself. Compare, they say, the present with the past— the actual amount (however far from adequate) of knowledge now existing with the density of ignorance which darkened the commencement of the century; compare the educational returns of 1818 (when the day scholars were as one to 17 of the population, and the Sunday scholars as one to 24) with the similar returns of 1833 (when the day scholars were as one to ll, and the Sunday scholars as one to nine), and with the recent Census of 1851 (when the former were as one to eight and a half, and the latter as one to seven and a half) f J and then say how much of this progress is attributable to the voluntary principle—the *exclusive* agent down to 1833—and how much to the State, whose operations, only then commenced, were, not pushed forward with activity till 1846. And although it may be true that ignorance has not been yet completely overtaken, still, it is maintained, the power which thus has been continually with rapid steps gaining on it would, if left alone, soon traverse the small intervening space.—And so, too, with regard to any advance in the *character* as well as in the *quantity* of education, voluntary effort would, it is contended, prove more efficacious in the long run than would Government inspection; since the former gives the utmost freedom to what hitherto has been the source of nearly all improvement, viz., individual enterprise and competition, while the latter, though Indeed, the design and hope of the voluntary party seems to be, that in course of time the assistance now afforded to the working classes may no longer be required; their habits being so improved, and their sense of duty so excited, that the whole community, except the truly pauper portion, will be *selMnstructed.*

See Evidence of Rev. J. H. Hinton, M. A., before the Manchester and Salford Education Committee, Session 1853.

"1640. *Chairman.*—If the religious bodies came forward with large subscriptions and established schools, do you mean that those schools are to be self-supporting amerwards, by school fees?—That would be my object: it in the object of tlie Congregational Board of Kducation and of the Voluntary School Association.

"1641. Your object would be, merely to establish a school, to raise the school building, to put the thing in working order, and then to leave it to shim for itself V—Not for itself absolutely, but to help it into a self-supporting condition, just as I would teach a little child to go alone.

"1652. You would have no permanent aid granted to parents?—None; that part of the system should be considered entirely temporary, and intended to issue in a state of things in which all parents should pay for the education of their own children. I would aim at bringing this part of the voluntary system to an end as soon as possible—its work being done.

"1658. *Sir George Grey.*—Do you anticipate that at an early period the parents of all classes of children in this country will be able to pay lor their own children?—There is rapid progress towards it." t These figures are not always quoted with the necessary qualification that the returns of 1818 and 1833 were much less perfect than those of 1851, and that, consequently, the rate of increase, (though undoubtedly, after all allowances, considerable) is not so great as thus appears. at first, perhaps, acute and innovating, would at length become inevitably slothful, and diffuse through all our educational agency the easy sluggishness of official torpor.—-And while thus superiority is claimed for voluntary effort in providing for improvements in the mode and matter of instruction, the effect upon the *general character* of those instructed must, it is considered, be incomparably more benignant under a free than under a State-endowed school-system; fostering—no unimportant part of education—those invaluable habits of selfdependence which, much more than aught besides, avail to form the future race of citizens industrious, provident, and free.

The *numerical* strength of this party is probably not inconsiderable. It comprises nearly the whole of the Congregational and Baptist bodies, (which together possess G,033 chapels and 1,820,103 sittings) and many members of the smaller sections of Wesleyan Methodists. The Friends too, for the most part, adhere to this standard.

Upon the other hand, the advocates of State assistance in the matter of Position of the education say that voluntary agency alone is not sufficient to supply the popular wants—that, in such circumstances, it is both the right and duty of the State to apply towards this end a part of its resources—and that nothing but desirable results can be anticipated from its intervention.

1. In estimating the extent of further effort necessary to provide the people with good education, those who urge a

State provision for this purpose draw their inferences less from figures showing present school accommodation and attendance than from certain prominent facts in every day experience, illustrating the actual condition of large classes of society. The prevalence of crime and vagrancy, and immorality—the almost universal ignorance of criminals and vagabonds—the number of marriages where one or other of the parties signs the register with a mark—the inferiority in information of the labouring classes in this country, as compared with those of several foreign countries;—these broad facts are held to indicate too clearly that great numbers of the English people must get either no instruction at all, or else so little or so bad as to be practically worthless. Not denying that the voluntary system has accomplished much within the present century, and that it might perhaps, in the course of years, accomplish very much more, it is contended that our need is much too urgent for delay, and that any procrastination dooms a multitude of children meanwhile to a certainty of ignorance and crime. The operations of voluntaryism also are, it is maintained, distinguished by a fitfulness that often perils the support of schools established by its means; thus showing that it cannot be relied upon to bear the additional burden requisite in order to secure their thorough and continual efficiency. It therefore, it is urged, devolves most naturally on the State—possessing the ability to render large and constant aid—to accelerate the speed at which we are progressing towards a state of things which shall be satisfactory and safe. 2. The existence of an educational deficiency being thus, it is supposed, established, and the *ability* of the State to meet the want assumed, the *right* of the State to interfere is vindicated principally on the ground that, as the effects of ignorance are *social* injuries, society must needs possess the right of selfdefence. If punishments for crime, it is urged, are only or chiefly to be justified because of their *preventive* influence, how can the State be reasonably hindered from employing for this end the much more efficacious instrument of education? To the argument that this involves the concession to the State of the right to interfere with any other preventive agencies—such as the pulpit and the press, the erection of better houses, and the payment of better wages—it is answered, that every case of interference must be judged upon its special merits be afforded for opposing such excess of interference when it is attempted. As to the objection, that the claim involves the application of the public money to religious teaching, one part of the friends of State provision do not consider that to be in any way objectionable, and the other part do not admit that such a consequence must necessarily result. 3. The advantages which would, it is anticipated, follow the appropriation of the public taxes to the furtherance of education, are considered by the advocates of such a measure to be so auspicious that any incidental disadvantages could weigh but little in comparison. But they are far from admitting that the evils apprehended by the voluntary party are inevitable or even probable. They think that the system may be so arranged that voluntary efforts may be fostered rather than discouraged, and that such extensive powers may be assigned to local parties that the fear of a *bureaucracy* need not be entertained. In confirmation of their views, they point to actual experience as shown in the United States; whose people, more intelligent perhaps than those of any European country, cannot certainly be said to be less self-reliant or less free.

These are the two *great* educational parties into which the friends of popular enlightenment are now divided. But the latter of these two is itself divided into three subordinate parties, whose divergence from each other has relation to the mode in which the State should exercise the influence which all of them agree that it should have. These parties are—the Committee of Council on Education, which dispenses the existing grants; the party favourable to a Local Rate applied to aid the schools of all religious bodies; and the Secular Party, advocating local rates applied to secular teaching only. The source of all these parties will be found to be the difficulty of dealing, in any plan of State interposition, with the *religious* element in education.

tfPriwCcn4ncil Committee o *Frivj* Council has been gradually developed from a rather humble origin to its present large dimensions, mainly by fortuitous events, and principally by the legislative failures which demonstrated the inability of Government to carry any large and comprehensive measure. It was then perceived, that if the State was to act at once and efficiently in promoting education, it was only through the medium of this Committee that its operations could be carried on. Accordingly, the plans of the Committee were elaborated and the funds at its command progressively augmented, till they reached, in 1853, the annual amount of 260,000/. That this amount will be increased still further seems to be inevitable, unless speedily some *national* measure be adopted; for the schemes already sanctioned and the obligations virtually contracted cannot otherwise be prosecuted and fulfilled.—In making grants, the Committee recognises all religious creeds, and advances funds in aid of local contributions to all such as will submit to its inspection. Practically, however—as the Congregational and Baptist Bodies almost universally decline to accept the public money, and the comparative poverty of many of the other bodies of Dissenters hinders them from raising from their own resources the proportion necessary to procure assistance—nearly nine-tenths of the annual grant are given to the Established Church.f " The whole of the calculations contained in Chapter III., as to the demand for the supply _ of now teachers, the power of the Training Colleges to absorb the supply of Queen's scholars;' and the increase of the number of assistant teachers, depend on the support of the present rate of progress, which could not be accomplished without a corresponding increase in the Parliamentary grants. The whole machinery of the Training Colleges, and of the apprenticeship and Queen's scholarships, would come to a dead lock if this aid were withdrawn, and would be almost fatally embarrassed without its increase."— Public Education, 4c., by Sir James Kay Shuttleworth, Bart. t The Committee of Council may be said to have been singularly free from the charge of partiality in their administration of the public money. The only eases of complaint within my knowledge are two, which occurred in Wales, in 1861, in one of which the cause alleged is, that

The State party divided into three subordinate parties.

The fact, that while the Privy Council is in full activity, two other plans Objections urged should be in zealous agitation, seems to indicate a feeling in the public mind aeainst this P111that the present plan of State interposition is not altogether satisfactory, Objections are, indeed, preferred against it upon several grounds. Apart from the danger fancied to pertain to it as leading to a centralized control, and committing great and dangerous powers to the hands of Government inspectors—it is urged that, on a matter of such vast importance as the education of the people, legislation ought not to be exercised by the mere "minutes" of a board not practically subject to effective Parliamentary supervision. Its plan of operations also is objected to, as being, though ostensibly impartial, actually not so; since the taxes taken from the nation generally (nearly half consisting of dissenters) are appropriated in a vast preponderance to the schools of the Established Church. The fact that this is owing, not to any preference shown by the Committee, but to the refusal of assistance by some bodies and to the poverty of others, is not looked upon by Nonconformists as a satisfactory answer. It explains, they say, the *cause* of the inequality, but does not justify it—neither the possession by particular sects of conscientious scruples, nor their want of worldly wealth, affording any valid reason why they should be taxed to aid such other sects as may be both unfettered and rich. A similar objection is maintained by others, not dissenters, on the ground that, to make the distribution of the funds supplied by all depend upon the contributions of the few is to establish, by the very assistance of the State, an educational monopoly—to render help just where it is superfluous—and to make the tax least fruitful to the places and the persons most requiring aid. Of course, one principal ground of opposition by *dissenters* is that the public money ought not in any case to be applied to the support of *religious* teaching, and apparently they think it even more objectionable that the State should pay impartially for the teaching of several inconsistent creeds than that it should favour one, Upon the other hand, an influential portion of the Church of England,—represented in this matter by the National Society,— complains of the conditions by which grants to Church schools are restricted; just and reasonable liberty to local founders and supporters being, it is urged, denied them, by the stipulations as to management, insisted on by the Committee.!

The principal features of the present plan are these:—a fund derived from Common ground *general* taxation—administered by a *central* board—in *aid* of voluntary contri-twother " butions—to *all* religious bodies. Both of the other schemes agree in proposing schemes, the substitution of *local* for central taxation and control—the *entire* support of schools by rates, to the exclusion of voluntary aid—and a wholly *gratuitous* instruction. It appears to be considered by both parties that the practical adoption of these principles would remove the main objections which exist against the present system. By the substitution of a local rate and local when further school accommodation was contemplated for the parish of Llangefni (where full nineteen-twentieths of the poorer classes are dissenters), the Committee, amer determining that only one school was needed, refused to aid a British School, conducted ou an unsectarian basis, and awarded a grant to a national school, the management of which was to be necessarily in the hands of churchmen. But it seems that, on remonstrance, grants were ultimately made to *both* schools. —See Parliamentary Paper, Session 1852; No. 577.—"Correspondence between the Committee of Council on Educion and the Promoters of the National and British Schools at Llangefni, Anglesey, &c." The opportunity for this supervision occurs when the annual grant is proposed. The objection is, that this opportunity has been proved by experience to be insufficient—that it is confined to a single occasion in one House of Parliament—and that this mere inferential approbation of a minute, given hastily in one year, virtually compels assent in after years, since schemes involving future increase of expense may thus be sanctioned, without due consideration, by a money-vote, and succeeding Parliaments have only the alternative of augmenting the grant, or undoing what has been begun.

t See Correspondence between the Committee of Council and the National Society, Minutes of Council, 1847-U. Petition to both Houses of Convocation, July 1852.

P management for a national fund and a central board, it is thought that the danger of *bureaucracy* would be avoided; while, by throwing the whole burden on the rates, it is imagined that the fitfulness and partiality of voluntary effort would be superseded by a constant and unfailing bounty—raised, too, much more equitably than at present, since *all* would have to yield their proper contribution to the fund which now is levied wholly on the charitable few: That the schools maintained in this way should be *free* is deemed a necessary consequence of the rate, since that is supposed to be the form in which the schoolfee would be paid.

Objections to these common grounds.

The objections Urged against these common features of the two new schemes are chiefly felt by the voluntary party, who, in general, protest with equal strength against a local as against a central interference; their essential ground of opposition being, that to levy by compulsion what might else be rendered as a duty or a charity must needs prove highly detrimental to the character both of those who pay the rate in lieu of school-fees and of those who pay it in the stead of voluntary gifts; impairing, in the former case, the feeling of *parental,* in the latter case the sense of *Christian* obligation, and in place of these exalted motives substituting the inferior impulse of a mere obedience to human law. But, apart from these objections to the general principle of compulsion, by whatever power, local or national, applied, it is contended that to give *gratuitous* instruction will inevitably lessen in the popular esteem its value, and produce, as in Americaf, a very general and lamentable non-attendance. At the same time, it is argued, rate-sustained free schools will work enormous injury to private and to voluntary schools, which cannot long exist exposed to such unequal competition. And while thus involving all the disadvantages of free schools, they would not, it is contended, be *really* free; since the very classes Tho particular scheme of the Manchester and Salford party does not, indeed, Rive much authority to the local boards; but, undoubtedly, the tendency of public feeling is towards conferring on the parties who supply the funds the principal share in the management of the choofi.

t The complaints by the superintendents of common schools in the United States of absenteeism are most bitter. After mentioning that, in the State of Massachusetts, out of 204,436 children, between four and sixteen years of age, wholly or mainly dependent upon the common schools, there were no fewer than 42,960 in summer and 29,413 in winter who "were not brought for a day within the influences of the schools," the Report of Mr. Horace Mann goes on to say:— "But another, and a scarcely less deplorable phase of the subject remains to be presented. Many of those whose names were enrolled upon the register-book of the schools have a flagrant amount of absences to atone for. The average attendance in summer was but 123,046, and in winter but 143,878. Hence, of the 204,436 children, supposed to be dependent upon the common schools for their education, there was an *average* absence during summer of 81.390. and an *average* absence during winter of 60,558. In strictness, too, a still further reduction should be made from the number of attendants, both on account of the 3,656 children under four years of age who were enrolled in the summer schools, and on account of the 9,977 above sixteen years of age who were enrolled in the winter schools. But I forbear; for it cannot be necessary to add another repulsive lineament to the deformities of a picture already so frightful. Indeed, one would naturally say. beforehand, that such a likeness, copied year after year from a genuine and indisputable original, would prove too much to be borne by any one, did not experience demonstrate that there" must be about one quarterpart of the parents in Massachusetts whoso nervous tissue on this subject can bear anything."—Twelfth Annual Report of the Hon. Horace Mann, Secretary of the Hoard of Education (Massachusetts), 1849. From this it. appears that the average number in attendance compared with the number registered was 74 per cent. in summer and 76 per cent. in winter; and this is subject to some qualification on account of the mode of keeping the register. When it is recollected that tho number constantly attending, in England, as compared with the number on the books, is 79 per cent. in public schools and 91 per cent. in private schools, it will probably be considered a testimony in favour of our system, so far as *regularity of attendance* is concerned. And this impression would perhaps be deepened by a reference to the Returns of the State of New York (probably a better *average* State than Massachusetts), where, in 1850 and 1851, the attendance was as follows:— 1850. 1851. for whose use they are Supposed td be In chief established—those who are Said td be too indigent to pay a fee—would actually, through the rate (involving higher house-rent) be supplying more than an equivalent.

But these two plans, which have thus far common features, and are met with The two plans common objections, differ fundamentally upon the subject of *religious teaching.* mode of giving

The one, which was embodied (more or less completely) in the recent *Manchester jjf10"8 iustl'uc" and Salford Boroughs Education Bill,* insists upon the impartation, in all schools m, iii.. iiji T 2-*The Local* supported by the public money, ot religious knowledge. It appears to have *Denominational* been thought by those who favour this proposal, that a nation so impressed as is *artt-*

the English nation by a deep conviction of the vital import of religious training to the young would never sanction the appropriation of its funds to the maintenance of schools in which religious truth should not be inculcated. But desiring, at the same time, to preserve religious freedom, they decline to choose one special form of truth as that which should alone be taught; but offer due proportions of the rate to *every* religious body which at present has a day school on condition (as a guarantee for the religious teaching) that the Holy Scriptures in the authorified version shall be daily read, and with a further stipulation (as a guarantee for liberty of conscience) that no child shall be required, against its parents' wishes, to receive instruction in particular creeds or catechisms. Thus, it appears to them, the payers of the school-rate, comprehending persons of various religious principles, will obtain at once religious teaching and religious liberty: the tax procured frdm all will go to support the religious views of all.

The principal objection urged against this scheme is, that it offers no accept- objections able security for the rights of conscience. Roman Catholics, it is maintained, 2isUpSnagainst would be excluded by the stipulation for the authorified version of the Bible. The permission to a child to retire from school when instruction is to be given in any catechism would, it is contended, be inoperative, if the master might at any other time instruct the whole school in the *doctrines* of that catechism; and no words can be devised to hinder him from this which would not also prohibit *all* religious teaching. On the other hand, the National schools could not preserve their fundamental character if children taught in them were to be allowed to absent themselves from instruction in the catechism, and from attendance in the church; so that either the charter of the National Society must be infringed, or the National schools must be deprived of any portion of the rate. To Dissenters—who protest against all application of the public money to religious teaching—the proposal is open to the same objections which they bear against religious endowments altogether; and they say, that being conscientiously unable to receive the slightest portion of the rate, they would be forced to pay twice over—once to support their own schools, and again towards the maintenance of the schools of other sects. To many parties, amongst both churchmen and dissenters, the proposal to sustain with public money teachers of varying and hostile creeds appears distasteful, as compelling them to aid in propagating doctrines some of which they conscientiously believe to be erroneous, and which cannot be, by any possibility, all true.f See Bill for promoting Education in the Municipal Boroughs of Manchester and Salford; Tracts by Rev. C. Richson; Evidence before Parliamentary Committee, &c.

t This objection is thus put by Lord Mclgund. Ho Is speaking of the present systemj but his observations are equally applicable to the scheme proposed. "I cannot go so far as the Lords of the Privy Council and as tile Government of the country seem to have gone in regard to perfect liberty: for it seems to me that the toleration they propose is a sort or toleration carried to an extreme excess. It is toleration run mad. It is not merely that every individual shall have a right to follow out his own opinions on religion according to the manner ne thinks best, but that every opinion on religious subjects shall be paid by the State money. Why, under those Minutes of the Privy Council, you have the Free Church paid to oppose the Establishment, and the Establishment paid to oppose the Free Church. You have the Episcopal Church paid to oppose, I suppose, both the Free Church and the Establishment, and you have the Roman Catholic Chureh paid to oppose all three. In short, you have a system of payment and encouragement of every system of religion whatever, however monstrous or absurd it may be."—Speech S. *The Secular* A strong conviction of the existence of inextricable difficulties in the way of *2artv*-legislation on this subject, if the money raised from all the various sects toge ther were to be expended for religious teaching, so as to secure, upon the one hand, that religion should be *really* taught, and yet to preserve, upon the other hand, the rights of conscience—seems to have occasioned the proposal that the 'application of the common fund should be restricted to the purely *secular* instruction, with regard to which no difference of sentiment prevails. Accordingly, the *Secular Party* proposes that, without prohibiting in any school religious teaching, there shall be appointed *special times* at which it shall be given, and specific *other* times at which the *secular* instruction shall be given. By assisting with the rate the *latter* only—leaving the religious training either to the teacher at some other time, or else to the clergymen and ministers to whom belong the right and duty of such spiritual oversight—it is conceived that no one's conscience could be possibly offended, that a sound and useful education in all secular knowledge would be placed within the reach of all, and that religious culture would be amply and perhaps more truly realified when made an object by itself than when mixed up, as now, with what must be to a great extent incongruous and detrimental. It appears to them that no impediment whatever would be caused to the inculcation of religious truth by the exclusive impartation, at particular hours, of reading, writing, or geography—since the acquisition of such arts and knowledge cannot be regarded as involving any irreligious tendency. Indeed, it is asserted, this is the very plan adopted practically in nine-tenths of the private schools to which the middle and upper classes send their children; and a further test of experience is found in the case of the United States, whose people, probably inferior to none in their religious character, receive their education, almost universally, in schools of this description

The great objection urged against the secular plan is, that, although it contemplates nothing *hostile* to religion, it creates a necessity that the young shall be withdrawn, by force of law, from the reach of religious influences during a considerable portion of their educational career. It is held by the opponents of the scheme, that to form religious character requires, not only definite instruction, at particular times, in the various Christian doctrines, but a constant application of those doctrines in the ordinary routine of the school; and that positively to prohibit the instructor, when enforcing discipline or answering inquiries, from appealing to the highest sanctions and explaining most important truths, must necessarily deprive him of the greater portion of his influence and produce a bad effect upon the children. In short, it seems to be considered that, while there is a multitude of children whose sole chance of being influenced religiously is during their attendance at the elementary schools, such influence can only be exerted by a really religious teacher, constantly encouraging the most exalted motives; and that this desirable influence would be much weakened, and perhaps entirely lost, if either the appeal were made exclusively to a lower class of motives (as to those derived from merely *natural* religion), or the lesson were postponed to another time, or referred to another party.

Objections to this plan.

I adopt this appellation, as being generally used; but the party in question does not admit that it any the less aims:it a religious education than do others. t Sec Evidence before Parliamentary Committee on the Manchester and Salford Bill. "'National edi—:':' " papers read: T. M. Gibson,

Thus, at present, stands the educational question. Probably the principal effect upon the mind of an impartial witness of these various phases of the national sentiment, in reference to the means of popular enlightenment, must be a sense of the enormous difficulties which beset the path of legislation in this matter, if, upon the one hand, no invasion be permitted of religious liberty, while yet, upon the other, no indifference be shown towards religious truth. Nor does the economic difficulty seem less serious—how the State is to assist in providing schools without demoralizing parents, and without destroying competition. It is probably a lively appreciation of the latter obstacle which has hitherto prevented a provision from the public bounty for that very class whose vice and crime have been and are the strongest arguments for State assistance; for it certainly is not a little singular that those—the absolutely indigent—who have by every party (even by the voluntary) been committed to the care of the State, as properly sustaining towards them the relation of a parent, have been almost utterly unbenefited by the grants which Parliament has now for twenty years distributed. No doubt the neglect of these most urgent claimants must be owing to the practical difficulty of *defining* destitution and applying any *test* of poverty. The workhouse does, indeed, effectually indicate one portion, and the prison indicates another, but no valid test has yet been found by which to circumscribe the class, *outside* the workhouse and the jail, who may really be unable to provide the means of education for their children. And, no doubt, it has been strongly felt that to establish *free* schools, without some security that they should only be resorted to by.those who are in truth without the means of payment, would be to incur the very serious danger of destroying, in the class above, the feeling of parental obligation, and to enter on a course which *must,* as the schools are gradually filled by other than indigent children, be further and further trod indefinitely until all existing schools were overthrown. And then—to further complicate this almost hopeless entanglement—some persons, of no mean authority, have intimated their conviction that the class whose misdeeds are the grand incitement to the wish for State-interposition cannot be effectually reached by Governmental agency, nor otherwise than by the voluntary zeal of those who may be prompted to the task by Christian sympathy for these neglected outcasts.

Of course it is not here that any opinion is to be expressed, if any were entertained, upon the merits of the controversies which now agitate the public mind—endeavouring ardently to gain by safe and equitable means a vastly important end. It may, however, be permitted to reiterate a doubt respecting the success of any schemes to elevate the masses of the population by mere elementary instruction while the social circumstances of the multitude continue so unfriendly to their intellectual and moral progress. For the real educational calamity at present is—not that the children do not go to school, but that they stay at school for such a limited period; and this results directly from the want of adequate inducement to prolong their education in the face of opportunities for early labour. Doubtless many thousands of children would be kept at school, who are now at a very early age removed, if any great advantages from education were discernible by parents, as procuring either physical or intellectual enjoyment for the after-life. But must it not be, though reluctantly, allowed that they have only too much reason for their apathy? "Of what avail"—they may, and not unreasonably, ask— "can education be "to those who must, of sad necessity, reside in these impure and miserable "homes, from which, if it were possible, ourselves would be the first to flee? "Or what delight can education yield to those who, on emerging from the Expressions to this effect have been uttered by the Earls of Shamesbury and Harrowby, and byMr.M.D.HUl.Q.C.

"school, where taste has been acquired and appetite excited, find that both the f treasures and the sweets of literature are for beyond their reach *V* Such, really if not in words, are the much-too-reasonable questions by which parents, of the humbler ranks excuse their inattention to their children's education: they imagine they are doing just enough to fit them for their future and unalterable lot, and that all beyond would be at best but superfluity. What then is wanted to ensure a greater measure of success to present efforts? Surely, the creation of a more benignant *atmosphere.* However carefully the tree of knowledge may be planted, and however diligently tended, it can never grow to fruitfulness or beauty in an uncongenial air. Concurrently with all direct attempts to cultivate the popular intelligence, there needs to be a vigorous endeavour to alleviate, if not remove, that social wretchedness which blights all educational promise, and to shed around the growing popular mind an affluence of wholesome light on which the half-developed plant may feed and thrive.

Whatever restrictions, therefore, may by a proper delicacy be imposed upon the expression here of any opinion on the more immediate means to he adopted for promoting elementary instruction, it will not be out of place to advocate those indirect yet influential means which—whether they be movements on behalf of temperance, health, cleanliness, and better dwellings, or for public lectures, libraries, and cheap and wholesome literature f—must, by raising the the position of the people and by bringing within their reach the *fruits* of intellectual toil, inevitably tend to render education much more valued, and therefore much more sought. Apart from their own special objects, all these movements have a potent favourable action upon primary education; for the social elevation of the parents makes the adequate instruction of their offspring needful to their proper pride, while the cheap diffusion of information greatly multiplies the inducements to learning by multiplying greatly its rewards. However long may last the difficulties which now hinder any equitable scheme of *national* instruction, *here* at least there is ample and common ground for effort upon which both the public and the Legislature have appropriate parts to play. And if upon the cultivation of this wide and open field a greater amount of labour be expended, who shall say it is impossible that, in the course of some few years, before the Gordian knot which now perplexes statesmen and philanthropists could be untied, the people may themselves have severed it?

I must now, Sir, bring to a conclusion these remarks which, in obedience to your request, I have prepared as an introduction to the Educational Statistics. I am quite aware that they are very meagre and inadequate, compared with the importance and extent of the investigation. But, for various reasons, independently of unfamiliarity with the subject, this was unavoidable. The publication, at as early a period as possible, of the facts obtained by this inquiry, has been always felt to be above all else desirable; and the time devoted to the Preface, therefore, has been strictly limited to that which has been indispensably required for the publication of the Abstracts. It is now, too, absolutely necessary that this Census altogether, so unwillingly protracted, should be closed.

Mindful of your desire and purpose that the principal results of the late Enumeration should be made, much more than hitherto, available for *popular* _ One of the objects of the " Working Men's Educational Union" is the provision of a superior kind of lectures as a substitute for the ordinary amusements of the people.

t Much, undoubtedly, is doing even now in providing cheap literature; but a vast deal more remains to be accomplished — especially in the department of cheap *newspapers,* an abundance of which would probably do more to assist education than would several millions of money spent upon elementary schools without some such inducement for the people to attend them. information, I have not considered that the previous sketch of educational agencies, though superficial, would he altogether useless, nor abstained from introducing facts which, though well-known to many persons, may perhaps be new to most. It would, of course, be vain to hope that, in a work like this, the statements and the figures should prove wholly unimpeachable; the utmost that can be affirmed is, the existence of a disposition to be fair and the expenditure of pains to be correct. The gentlemen on whom more specially devolved the duty of preparing the succeeding Tables all bestowed upon their arduous task considerable ability and the greatest care. I am therefore led to hope that, notwithstanding certain unavoidable deficiencies, the accompanying Abstracts are so far complete and accurate that your original object in proposing this inquiry may appear to have been gained—that in this volume may be found collected ample *data* for determining those questions upon which the public mind has hitherto been dubious, and that many important facts may be revealed by which our present educational position may be clearly manifested and our future course directed.

Census Office, 25 March 1854.

I have the honour to be,
Sir,
Your very faithful Servant,
Horace Mann. SUMMARY TABLES.

The above figures show the statistics of all the Schools for which Returns have been received at the Census Office. But the Lists supplied by the Enumerators mention, in addition to the above, 1,206 other Day Schools (107 Public and 1,099 Private); and 877 other Sunday Schools, from which no Returns were procurable. Assuming that each of these unrepresented Schools contained, upon an average, us many Scholars as did each of the Schools which made Returns, and that the proportion of the sexes and attendants was the same, the ultimate result of the Educational Census will be this

Class III.—cont. *Denominational*—cont. Moravians Wesleyan Methodists-British „ *Others* Methodist New Connexion— *British* „ *Others* Primitive Methodists— AMI p *Others* Bible Christians- *British*
„ *Others*
Wesleyan Methodist Association-
Calvinistic Methodist s—
British
„ *Others*
Lady Huntingdon's Connexion--*British*
„ *Others*
New Church
Dissenters (not defined)
-*British*
„ *Others*
Lutherans-
French Protestants-
German Missionary Society
Isolated Consregations— *British*
    Roman Catholics
Jews-
    British
Others-
Class IV.
Ragged Schools *(exclusive of those supported by religious bodies)* §
Orphan Schools
Blind Schools
Deaf and Dumb Schools-
School for Idiots
Factory Schools
Colliery Schools
Chemical Works Schools
Foundry School
Mechanics' Institution Schools-w
Industrial Schools--
Agricultural Schools
Railway Schools-
Philanthropic Society's Farm School
Other Subscription Schools of no specific character

Total of British Schools of all Descriptions

has, a school for V
l, although tha t
"school" is here mca one range of building is..D
separate superintendence.
iought necessary to encumber these Tables with the number of scholars *attending* each class of day schools. The all privHte schools and the aggregate of public schools is given in the previous summary (Table A.); and thero ho conclusion that the proportion of attendance is materially greater in one class of public schools than in given respecting two counties; *port,* page ltx.

'"classification of these schools, see Supplement I. to Tahlo B., pag# 02.

Supplement III. to Table B.

Showing a Number of Schools which, though included in Table B. amongst those in Classes III. and IV. (as being *principally* maintained by Subscriptions) are yet, in some degree, also assisted by *Endowments*. The test by which Schools supported by, a mixture of endowments and subscriptions were, in the General Summary, included or excluded from Class II. was—whcther the income from endowments exceeded or fell short,of the income from subscriptions. Consequently in Table B. Class II. does not completely represent the number of Schools which derive support, in greater or less degree, from endowments. The Table given above is designed to show what number of Schools must be added to Class II. in Table B. if it be desired to ascertain how many aro *in any degree* assisted by endowments. The result appears to be that the total number of Schools receiving some kind, of endowment (exclusive of Collegiate and Grammar Scuooib) is 3455, containing 281,904 scholar; (169,570

Table C.—*continued*. Table D. Table F.

Endowment of Public Schools. Number of Schools having Endowments of particular amounts.

Table E.

TEACHERS IN PUBLIC SCH00LS. SUMMARY OF ENGLAND AND WALES, each of the under-mentioned Branches of Learning. EWCIAND AITD WALES. The first of these three Tables shows the aetual result of the information given in the Returns which were complete upon this point. The second shows an estimate for the total number of Scholars, proceeding on the assumption that the cour.e of tuition in the Schools which sent incomplete Returns was the same as that pursued in the Schools which sent complete Returns. The third exhibits the *proportion* which the number of Scholars instructed in each branch bears to 100 of the whole number of Scholars.

Table H.

Ages, in Quinquennial Periods, of 1,450,504 Scholars concerning whom the Information was given.

This Tahle has been constructed with reference to *R'gistration* Counties; but the proportions here contained may be applied to the totals of the Counties proper as shewn in Table O. *post*. For a comparison of the ages of Scholars in Public and Private Schools respectively, see Table M, pae 107.

Table I.

Dates At Which Existing PUBLIC SCHOOLS.

This Table does not. of coarse. displny the number of Schools existing at former periods, except very vaguely; since many existing were first established, since some, though established lsng ago, may have given the data of a new building or an *sparged* one, erected or enlarged

Table K.—*continued*.

Table L.

Showing, with respect to the Two Registration-Counties of Lancaster and Lincoln, the proportion of Scholars *attending* Day Schools as compared with the number On The Books; distinguishing the different *classes* of Schools.

Table M.

Ages, in Quinquennial Periods, of Scholars in Public and Private Day Schools respectively, in the Counties of Lancaster and Lincoln.

Table O.—*continued*.

Table O.—*continued*.

Table 0.—*continued*.

Table O.—*continued*. Table O.—*continued*.

Table O.—*continued*.

Table P.

NUMBER OF DAY SCHOOLS AND SCHOLARS IN THE PBINCIPAX BOROUGH8 AND LARGE TOWN8. 1'.iiisroL.—Parts only of th' Parishes of St. James with St. Paul, Westbury-upon-Trym, and Bedminster, ore withia the City of Bristol but the Schools and Scholars of the whole:ire here included. The population of the added parts is 2,555.

Table P.—*continued*. Halifax.—Parts only of the Townships of Southowram and Northowram are *i* cholaru of the whole arc heie included. The population of the added parti is 14,244. within the Borough of Halifax, but the Schools and

» Hull.—Part only of the parish of Sutton is within the Borough of Hull, but the Schools and Scholars of the whole are here included. The population of the added part is 859. .

t Ipswich.—Parts only of the parishes of Bramford, Sproughton, Westerfield, "Whitton-cum-Thurlston, and Rush mere, are within the Borouph of Ipswich, but the Schools and Scholars of the whole are here included. The population of the added parts is 2,101). :

Leeds.—Parts only of the townships of Tern pie news am and Seacroft are within the Borough of Leeds, but 4he Schools and Scholars

Table P.—*continued*.

Table P.—*continued*. Table P,—*continued*. Stockport.—Parts only of the Townships of Heaton Norris and Brinnington are within the Borough of Stockport, but the Schools and Scholars of the whole are here included. The population of the added pams is 2,238. f Sunderland.-Part only of the Township of Bishop Wearmouth is within the Borough of Sunderland, hut the Schools and Scholars the whole are here included. The population of the added part is 776. (I Swansea.-Parts only of the Parish of Llansamlct and of the Hamlet of Clane are within the Borough of Swansea, but the Schools and Scholars of the whole arc here ineluded. The population of th' added parti is *4,OP.7.*

Table P.—*continued*. DAY SCHOOLS
PUBLIC DAY SCHOOLS-
PRIVATE DAY SCHOOLS

Classification of Public Schools.

Class I.—Supported By Genebax Or Local Taxation-

Class II.—Supported By Endowments

Class III.—Supported By.. Religious Bodies

Class IV.—Otheb Public Schools...

Class I. Military School...

Prison School...

Workhouse Schools

Class II.

Collegiate and Grammar Schools

Other Endowed Schools

Class III. *Denominational.*

"Ch. of England—*National*, *Others*
Independents— *British* -
„ *Others* -
Society of Friends
Unitarians
Wcsleyan Methodists—
British -
„ *Others*
Roman Catholics
Class IV. 'Ragged Schools
'Orphan Asylum School
Factory School-
Other Subscription Schools of no specific character.
Table P.—*continued*. (entire Metropolis.)
Population, 2,862,236.
Class IV.—Other Public Schools-
Class I.
Workhouse Schools
Military Schools
Naval Schools
Prison Schools
Class II.
Collegiate and Grammar Schools
Other Endowed Schools
Class III.
Denominational. CChurch of England—
National
Others IJ Church of Scotland—
British m
m'
I co
„ *Others*
Presbyterian Church in, England Consisting of the 30 Registration Districts, in Middlesex, Surrey, and Kent, which comprise the Registrar-General's BUIn of Mortality. Table Q. Table R.
SUNDAY SCH0OLS, SCH0LARS, AND TEACHERS. SUMMARY Or ENGLAND AND WALES, SUNDAY SCH0OLS AND SCH0LARS IK THE PEINCIPAL B0R0UGHS AND LARGE T0WNS It has not been found possible to give the figures in all ea«es for the precise limits of Boroughs the boundary lines of which intersect parishes or townships. In these eases the schools and scholars lor the whole of such intersected parishes or townships have been included, and a note states w hat population should be added to that inserted in the heading; which is always the exact population of the t Ashton-under-lyne.—Part only of the Parochial Division of Audenshaw is within the Borough of Ashton-under-Lyne, hut the schools and scholars of the whole are here included. The population of the added part is 4.542.
: RrlsTot.IV.rts only of the Parishes of St. James with St. Paul, Westbury-up-on-Trym. and Bedminstcr, are within the City of Bristol, but the schools and scholars of the whole are here included. The population of the added parta is 2,555.
Bent Part only of the township of Elton is within the borough of Bury, but the schools and scholars of the whole are here included. The population of the added part is 1,000.
t Halifax.-Parts only of the townships of Southowram and Northowrani are. within the borough of Halifax, bat the schools and Hull.—Part only of the parish of Sutton is within the borough of Hull, but the schools and scholars of the whole are here included. The population of the added part is 859. t Tmwirn — Parts onlv of the parishes of Brnmford, Sprouphton Westerfleld. Whitton-cum-Thurlston, and Rushmcre are within the borough of Ipswich, but the schools and scholars of the whole are here included. The population of the added parts is 2,100. Leeds-Parts only of the townships of Templenewsam and Seacroft are within the borough of Leeds, but the schools and scholars of the whole are here included. The population of the added parts is 2,539. 5 Leicester.—Part only of the parish of St. Margaret is within the Borough of Leicester, hut the schools and scholars of the whole nre here included. The population of the added part is 494. II Liverpool —Parts only of Toxteth Park and of the parish of West Derby are within the borough of Liverpool, but the schools and scholars ol the whole are here included The population of the added parts is 12,364. % Macclesfield.—Parts only of the townships of Hurdsneld and Sutton are within the borough of Macclesfield, but the schools and scholars oif the whole are here included. The population of the added parts is Vl Merthyr Tydfil.— Parte only of the Parishes of Merthyr TydOl and Vainor are within the Borough of Heritor Tydfil.' but tho Stockport.—Parts only of the townships of Ileaton-Norris and Brinnington are within the borough of Stockport, hut the schools and scholars nf the whole arc here included. The population ot'tbe added parts *a 2J£3i*. t Sunderland.—Part only of the township of Bishop-Wearmouth is within the borough of Sunderland, but the scbools and scholars of the whole are here included. The population of the added part is 776. « Z Swansea.—Parts nnly of the parishes of Llansamlet and of the hamlet of Clase are within the borough of Swansea. but the schools and scholars of the whole are here included. The population of the added parts in 4,007. Being the Mctropolitan portions of Middlesex, Surrey, and Kent within the limits adopted by the Registrar-General for the weekly bills
Table T.
SUBJECTS TAUGHT IN EVENING SCHOOLS FOR ADULTS. PARLIAMENTARY RETURN (No. 487, Session 1853,) showing 18 18. ,—Returns of the Number of Day Schools and Sunday Schools, and of the Number of to the "Parochial Returns made to the Select Committee appointed to inquire into the Education "Endowed and Unendowed Day Schools;" and also the "New Schools, Dame Schools, and Numher of Children " Educated Gratuitously, and those who paid for their Instruction." 1 8 3 3. II.—Returns of the Number of Day Schools and Sunday Schools, and of the Number of to the " Answers and Returns ma'de pursuant to an Address of the House of Commons, dated 'Infant Schools and Daily Schools, with the Number of their Scholars respectively, and the Number of Children in each Class of Schools of which the "Maintenance" is specified. the extent of Education in 1818, 1833, and 1851 respectively. -.--1818.
Day Scholars and Sunday Scholars, in England And Wales, in the Year 1818, acording of the Poor, Session 1818," with the estimated Population for the

Month of May 1818; distinguishing Ordinary Schools," with the Number of Children taught therein respectively; and also stating the figures for the Counties of Berks, Somerset, and Suffolk; the numbers which appear to be correct arc here inserted. An Appendix to the others refer to the details of Schools previously mentioned in general. It has not been found. practicable to make any satisfactory correction of --.-- 1 8 3 3.

Day Scholars and Sunday Scholars, in England And Wales, in the Year 1833, according the 24th day of May 1833," with the estimated Population for the Month of May 1833, distinguishing Sources of "Maintenance" of the Infant and Daily Schools and of the Sunday Schools, and the ---Comparison between 1818, 1833, and 1851.

Number of Day Scholars and Sunday Scholars, in England and Wales, in the Years 1818, the Day Scholars and Sunday Scholars respectively bore to the Population in each of those Years.

number of Scholars was not stated; the above numbers of Day Scholars and Sunday Scholars respectively include an estimate for these the previous years, it should be borne in mind that the Returns obtained in 1818 and in 1883 (especially those of lt&i) were much Ifltl complete few insignificant alterations, which havo been carried into the above Table (III).

Population of England and Wales at each Year of Age from Birth to 15.

This series was obtained by interpolation: the numbers being distributed over the respective ages so that they agree with those enumerated at each quinquennial age. It is believed, however, that the numbers at the first year or two are too few. ABRIDGMENT OF Me. HORACE MANN'S REPORT

ON EDUCATION IN SCOTLAND.

TO GEORGE GRAHAM, Esq. S*f*C. S*f*c. *fy*c. REGISTRAR-GENERAL OF BIRTHS, DEATHS, AND MARRIAGES.

Sir,

The following pages contain the tabulated results of the inquiries prosecuted at the Census of 1851 with respect to the Educational Establishments of Scotland.

Yielding to an urgent representation from that country that immediate publication is extremely desirable, you have resolved to present this volume without further delay. It has consequently been found to be impossible to furnish any introductory remarks of the character of those which accompany the English Tables; and the present preface must be limited to such explanations as appear to be essential to an accurate estimation of the figures.

In the first place it is necessary to state that the statistics are not complete; and that no means are in your possession of computing the extent of the deficiency. The efFect of the instruction given to enumerators—that the inquiry was a *voluntary* measure—was much more awkward in Scotland than in England; the enumerators were less careful, after this announcement, to deliver forms, and parties were less willing to supply the information. The absence, likewise, of a staff of local officers within the sphere of your own influence (as are the Registrars in England) prevented any attempt, like that made here, to supply, by subsequent inquiries, such deficiencies as really became apparent.

The total number of scholars in *Day Schools* respecting which information has been forwarded was 368,517. This gives a proportion to the population of Scotland (2,888,742) of 1276 per cent. , or one scholar to every 7'84 inhabitants. Making a fair allowance for deficient returns, it seems probable that about 14 per cent. (or 1 in 7) of the people of Scotland are at school. The number who, in answer to the question as to *Occupation,* on the *Householders' Schedule,* were Day Schools. returned as " Scholars," was 426,566. This source of information, it is true, is not entirely satisfactory; since so much is left to the judgment of the parents, whose conception of a " Scholar" might not correspond with what is generally meant to be conveyed by the term. Still, the information may be useful as supplying *some* assistance towards an estimate of the extent to which the present Educational Census of Scotland is deficient. The following Table presents a comparison of the figures gathered from *both* sources of intel

An attempt has been made to classify the Day Schools in four groups according to a distinction which prevails in the sources from which they are maintained. Class I. is designed to represent the number of schools which depend for their support upon the public taxes, whether national or local; and in this class all the Parochial and Burgh Schools have been placed. The object proposed by Class II. was to show the number of schools sustained in chief degree by *permanent endowment;* but it was found that in the returns the word "Endowment" was used to signify, not merely funds assigned in perpetuity for education (mortifications), but also the aid afforded by the Educational Societies, and the contributions of the heritors. An attempt to distinguish mortifications from the other kinds of endowment failed; so that the "Endowed Schools" in Class II. will represent the number (exclusive of Burgh and Parochial Schools) which derive the principal portion of their sustenance from endowments of the sort intended by the parties who prepared the returns. Class III. will show the action of *Religious Bodies* in the matter of Education, so far as they act denominationally; while Class IV. displays the influence of *general philanthropy,* apart from any sectarian organization. The Summary of Scotland, according to this view, appears in Table A. *(post,* p. 156); and the Supplements to that Table (on page 158) will afford facilities for making any other classification which may seem to be advisable.

The other tables of Day Schools refer to their *Income* (Table C.); the *character of Instruction afforded* (Tables D. and E,); the number of *Teachers* (Table E.); the *remuneration of Teachers* (Table G.); the *dates* at which schools were established (Tables H. and I.); and the *Ages* of the scholars (Table K).

Sabbath Schools. In the department of Sunday or Sabbath Schools there is not so much activity in Scotland as in England; for, while in the latter country the number of Sunday Scholars is 2,407,642, being 13'4 per cent. of the population, in Scotland (making, however, no allowance for defective and missing Returns,) the number is but 292,549, being only 10-1 per cent; of the population. The principal contributors amongst the Denominations are the following:— Table D. Table D.

No. of Scholars,
Established Church---76,233
United Presbyterian Church--54,324
Free Church---91,328
Independents----12,593
Wesleyan Methodists... 5,124
Roman Catholics -13,015

The Evening Schools for Adults form an interesting feature of the educa- Evening Schools tional condition of Scotland. Returns were received from 438 of such schools, for Adults containing 15,071 scholars.

Information was. obtained respecting 221 Literary, Mechanics, and other Literary and -i T Scientific Iuati

Bimilar Institutions.. tutions, &c.

However brief and hurried this Report, an acknowledgment must not be omitted of the important service rendered at the time of the Census by John Cay, Esq., Sheriff of Linlithgow, who, besides imparting much valuable information, revised the various forms, and adapted them to the state of things in Scotland.

I have the honour to be,
Sir,
Your most obedient Servant,
15 March 1854. Horace Mann.
  Class L
  Burgh Schools
  Parochial Schools
  Government Schools of Design t
  Military Schools---
  I'rison School
  "Workhouse Schools-
  Other Government Schools Class II.
Endowed Schools...
  Class III.
  Established Church
Reformed Presbyterian Church
United Presbyterian Church
Froo Church
Episcopal Church
Independents or Congrcgationalists

Baptists....
LRoman Catholics...
  Class IV.
  Bagged Schools *(exclusive of those supported by Religious Bodies)%*
Orphan Schools-
  Blind School
  Deaf and Dumb Schools....
Benevolent Society's School
Dumfries Education Society's School
Friend Society's School
Gaelic Society's Schools---
Industrial Schools.....
Factory Schools.....
Colliery Schools-
  Iron Works Schools....
Trades' Schools....
Seamen's Friend Society....
New Lanark Institution....
House of Refuge-
Other Subscription Schools, of no specific character-
205,318 163,169 173,330 161,754
43,594
232,442
78,000
58,007
22,100
62,715
18,932
135,043
38,287

By the term " School" is here meant a distinct Establishment. Thus a School for Boys and Girls, if under one general management and conducted in one range of Buildings,is regarded as only one School, although the tuition maybe carried on in separate compartments of the Building under separate superintendence.

In these Schools only Drawing and kindred subjects are taught; and the Scholars are mostly adults. Of the whole number of... Scholars. 21)4 were upwards of 15 years of age. J The total number of Ragged Schools is 21, containing 1077 scholars (1182 males and 7S5 females).

Table B.
SABBATH SCH00LS. (Classified according to the Denominations which support them.)
Showing the total number of Schools supported *in any decree* by Religious Bodies. (Exclusive of Parochial and Burgh Schools.) iVote.-The test by which schools supported by a mixture of endowments nnd subscriptions were, in the General Summary (Table A.), referred to Class II., or to either of the other elasses, was, whcther the income from endowments exceeded or fell short of the ineome from subscriptions; consequently, in the Summary (Table A.), Class II. does not completely represent the number of schools which derive support *inyreatcror less degree* from ENdOWMENT8, nor does Class 11I. completely represent the number of schools which derive support *in great'r or less degr'e* from Religious Bodies. The Tables on this page are designed so give this view.

For an explanation of the meaning of the term "Endowment" in these Tables, see Beport. Table C

Income Of Public Day Schools.
Number of Schools in which Instruction is SUMMARY OF SCOTLAND....
given in various Branches of Learning. . .. SUMMARY OF SCOTLAND.
Table E.
in various Branches of Learning. OF SCOTLAND. IN GIRLS' SCHOOLS. DESCRIPTION op SCHOOLS. DAY SCHOOLS PUBLIC DAY SCHOOLS PRIVATE DAY SCHOOLS *Classification of Public Schools.* Class I.—Sl'pported By General Or Local Taxation...
Clas9 Ii.—Supported By Endowments
  Class III.—Supported By Religious Bodies
  Class IV.—Othee Public Schools...
  Class I.
  Burgh Schools-
Parochial Schools.
Government Schools »
Military Schools
Prison School---
Workhouse Schools
Class II.
Endowed Schools
Class III.
Established Church
Reformed Presbv. Ch.-
J United Presby. Ch.
g J Free Church
  Episcopal Church-

Independents
Baptists-
Human Catholics-
   Class IV.
   Ragged Schools *(exclusive of those supported by lieli-f)ious Bodies)*
Orphan Schools-
Blind Schools...
Deaf and Dumb Schools
Benevolent Society's School
1-Himfriey Education Society's School
   Friend Society's School--
Gaelic Society's School
Industrial Schools
Factory Schools-
Colliery Schools
Iron Works Schools
Trades Schools-
Seaman's. Friend Society's School-
New Lanark Institution
House of Refuge
Other Subscription Schools of no i _
   Table F.
   Number of Teachers in Public Schools. *Classification of Public Schools.*
   Class I.—Supported By General Or Local Taxation-
   Class II—Supported By Endowments
   Class III.—Supported By Religious Bodies
   Class IV.—Other Public Schools
   Class I.
   Burgh Schools
Parochial Schools
Government Schools
Military Schools
Prison School
Workhouse Schools
Class II.
Endowed Schools
   Class III.
f Established Church Reformed Presby. Ch. fl United Presbyterian Ch. j J Free Church s' Episcopal Church c Independents
Baptists--
LRoman Catholics-
Class IV.
   Ragged Schools *(exclusive of those supported by Religious Bodies)*
   Orphan Schools
   Blind School
   Deaf and Dumb Schools
   Benevolent Society's School
   Dumfries Education Society's School
   Friend Society's School
   Gaelic Society's Schools
   Industrial Schools
   Factory Schools
   Colliery Schools
   Iron works Schools
   Trades' Schools
   Seamen's Friend Society's School...
   New Lanark Institution
   House of Refuge
   Other Subscription Schools, of no specific character
   Table G.
REMUNERATION OF TEACHERS IN PUBLIC SCHOOLS. SUMMARY OF SCOTLAHD.
Table K.
   Showing, in quinquennial Periods, the Ages of 286,611 Scholars concerning whom information
on the point was given.
   Table L.
   Endowments Of Public Schools. Number Of Schools Having Endowments Of
   Particular Amounts.
   Table M.
8ABBATH SCHOOL8 AND TEACHER8. (Classified according to the Denominations which support them.) SUMMARY OF SCOTLAND. 1—..
Unitarians--
   'Wesleyan Methodists:
Original Connexion
Primitive Methodists -
Independent Methodists
Wesleyan Reformers --
   New Church....
   Evangelical Union
   Isolated Congregations:
City Mission ...
Various ...
No Particular Denomination
Denomination not stated -
Reformed Protestant Congregation
All Evangelical Denominations
Christian Chartists
Free Gospel Church -.
Christian Brethren ---
Free Christian Brethren

Calton Association-
Bridgeton Association-
Sabbath School Union
Protestant ....
Unsectarian -
A Christian Congregation
Second Congregational
Church of Christ ...
   Other Chbibtiau Chtochbs:
Roman Catholics-
Jews ....
109 30
6
2
10 1 11
1
124 50 225 383 140
3
1
It will be sufficiently apparent that in erected in which the School wai held. t date given in thia Table appliei to the period when the I APPENDIX. EXPLANATORY NOTES
A8 TO THE MODE OF PROCURING AND DIGESTING THE RETURNS. APPENDIX. ENGLAND AND WALES.
MODE OF PROCURING AND DIGESTING THE RETURNS.

The object of the following remarks will be to show precisely the manner in which the original returns respecting education were procured—the obstacles which intervened to threaten incompleteness—the proceedings taken to remove those obstacles— the measure of success which followed these proceedings—and the various processes of tabulation and of estimates through which the returns themselves have passed in order to produce the results now published in the shape in which they are presented. Though not, probably, of general interest, such an explanation will be found of the utmost service to statistical inquirers, who, without such details, would be frequently unable to assign to the whole investigation and to special inferences the exact particular value, neither more nor less, to which they are entitled.

The machinery by which the General Census was accomplished is by this time probably familiar to most persons. England and Wales were divided into

30,610 small sections, each containing on an average 100 houses, but the rural sections having generally a less, and the urban sections generally a greater number. To each of these sections an Enumerator was appointed, with a mission to every house and separate tenement within his section. Upon two distinct occasions was this visit to be made; the first, in the course of the week ending Saturday, 29th March 1851, for the purpose of leaving a "householder's schedule" and explaining its requirements; the second, on the 31st March 1851, for the purpose of receiving the same schedule properly filled up or else of filling it up himself from the information of the inmates, This was the *general* census—of the numbers, sexes, ages, birthplaces, and occupations of the people.

These two opportunities (occurring only once in every ten years) of simultaneous communication with the occupants of every house in England, were seified upon in order to procure intelligence respecting *Education.* Forms were prepared (see copies *post),* containing questions to be answered by the heads or keepers of all *Day Schools, Sunday Schools, Evening Schools for Adults*—and *Literary and Scientific Institutions.*

The Enumerator was instructed on his first visit at a house, to inquire if a school of any sort was carried on there: if there was, a form was to be left to be filled up ready for his second visit on the Monday following. After this first visit and delivery of forms, the enumerator was to make a *list* of all the schools within his district, stating the names of the parties to whom the forms had been delivered. This list was at once deposited with the next superior officer, the Registrar (of whom there are 2190 in England and Wales), who would use it as a check upon the number of returns to be received from that enumerator. The forms for Sunday schools were either left at all the places of worship within the compass of the Enumerator's section, or delivered at the residence of some party ascertained to be officially connected with them. If these parties lived beyond the limits of the section, the communication was effected by the Registrar.

When thus delivering the forms, the Enumerator notified to those receiving them *thflt* they were not *compellable* to furnish information: it was left entirely to their option.

On the 31st of March, all over England, the forms were called for and collected. A refusal was of rare occurence. When collected, they were sent at once to the Registrar, who compared them with the lists in his possession, and, when made as perfect as was possible, despatched them and the lists to the Census Office.

And Walks. APPENDIX TO REPORT:— EXPLANATORY NOTES. 175

Towards the end of April, 1851, a vast confused accumulation of returns and lists had arrived. Most of the parcels, insecurely packed, had been forced open in the course of their transmission through the post, and the greater portion of 100,000 documents were intermingled, so that forms of different descriptions and from different localities were mixed together. This involved a process of *sorting*—forms of similar character (as referring to Day Schools or Sunday Schools, &c.) being brought together, and the whole then numbered and arranged and bound in topographical parochial order.

The next proceding was, to test the completeness of the results obtained. This test consisted in a careful comparison of the *lists* of schools with the school *returns,* in order to see whether for every school mentioned in the lists a corresponding return had been received. It was then discovered that some thousand or more of *lists* had not been sent. Communications, therefore, were despatched to the local officers, and by their aid, the missing lists, or substitutes for them, were procured. Upon comparing with the lists thus made complete the actual returns received, it was discovered that several thousands of schools, referred to in the lists, had not supplied returns: fresh applications, therefore, to the local officers were necessary. After much exertion and delay, a definite account was rendered of all the schools occurring in the lists, from some (principally private day-schools) no information could be got; but from most an answer was supplied. The number noticed as having thus declined to afford intelligence was 1583 (viz. 1206 Day-Schools and 377 SundaySchools); but doubtless this does not express the whole.

The returns being thus made as complete as possible, the tabulation of the facts was next proceeded with. The most essential items of intelligence were tabled, in parochial order, in Registration Districts or Poor Law Unions; the facts from each school return occupying a line. The tabling of Day schools was conducted in duplicate as to the more important entries, and particularly as to the *number of scholars,* and the two series, on their completion, were compared—by which means an important check was established and considerable accuracy, it is hoped, secured.

The returns, of course, were not all perfect. Many while giving full intelligence on one point overlooked another. Thus, sometimes, the number of the scholars *mi the books* being given, the number *in attendance* was omitted; sometimes, on the other hand, the number in attendance was supplied, but the number on the books not stated The course adopted, to obtain an uniformity in the returns, was to supply these vacancies by estimates; assuming that the proportion between the scholars on the books and those in attendance was the same in these particular instances as in the other schools for which complete returns were made. On examination of these full returns, the proportion of scholars in attendance as compared with the number on the books was found to be, in private day-schools 91 per cent, in public dayschools 79 per cent, and in Sunday schools 75 per cent. These proportions, therefore, were applied to the incomplete returns. This plan was adopted both for Day and Sunday Schools.

Again; on some occasions, while the *total* number of scholars was mentioned the proportion of the *sexes* was left undistinguished. Sometimes the scholars were distributed into boys, girls, and infants—the last being treated as if belonging to a third description of sex. In all these cases—if no indication was apparent on the face of the return that the school was adapted only for one sex— it was assumed that the scholars were equally divided into boys and girls. This plan was adopted both for Day and Sunday Schools.

These were the only interpolations. In all other cases, where imperfect information was supplied, as in the case of teachers, ages, income, subjects of instruction, &c, the plan has been to present in the Summary Tables only the perfect portion as a fair criterion of the whole; but, with reference to the *number* of scholars, it appeared essential to give something which might be accepted as the whole, and this could only be accomplished by the process thus described. The figures thus obtained by estimation were inserted in the Tables in *red ink,* in order to distinguish them from the authentic figures, and to show, by the extent to which the process was pursued, of computation. On reviewing these interpolations it may confidently be asserted that their number in proportion to the total number of entries is so small that no disturbance of the slightest consequence can have been caused, even if the estimate was not in every case accordant with the real though unknown fact

It was found that some of the schools returned as day schools, contained *adults*— persons upwards of twenty years of age: these were principally military schools, prison schools, &c. As it seemed advisable, on various grounds, to confine the view to schools for *juvenile* scholars, the adults in such establishments have been deducted, leaving only children and young persons in the tables. This course also has been followed with respect to schools for *secondary* education, such as schools of art, &c, as the scholars in such institutions would have probably already passed through their career of primary instruction, and ought not therefore to be mingled in one view with children in the elementary schools. It is possible that this elimination may have been in some few instances through oversight omitted, as the tables still include above 5,000 scholars upwards of twenty years of age; but *in general* this process has been carried out.

Whenever an opportunity occurred for comparing the census returns with statements from extraneous sources, this was done. By this means was discovered a considerable deficiency of *Workhouse Schoob.* The larger workhouses were not included in the districts of the ordinary enumerators—the returns of inmates being made by the masters; hence it happened that they were not furnished with the forms of school-returns. In order to supply the deficiency resulting from this cause, recourse was had to the accounts of average school attendance, in 1851, published by the Poor Law Board.

As a further means of showing what was the course adopted in digesting the Day School returns, the Instructions, in conformity with which this process was pursued, are here inserted: /

Instructions for the Classification and further Revision of Public Day Schools (on the Tables of A 2.)

The expression "Public " Schools is intended to apply to all schools supported, in *any degree,* from other sources than the payments by the scholars, and which are established in any degree for other objects than pecuniary profit to the promoters.

All schools which derive their income *solely* from such paymem, or which are maintained with a view to pecuniary advantage, are to be considered "Private" schools, whatever may be their sifie or educational character, and whether belonging to a single individual or to a large proprietary body.

Public schools, as thus defined, are to be classified according to The Different Agencies By Which They Are Established And Maintained, so as to present a view of the various distinct sources from which the existing educational provision of the country is supplied.

The *primary* classification will consist of *four* groups, as follow:
L Schools established and supported by Public.taxation, whether General or Local.
II. Schools established and supported principally by Endowments.
HL Schools established and supported principally by Religious Bodies.
rV. Other Public Schools, not embraced in the preceding classes.

I The *first* group will consist of schools connected With the various state estab-« lishments, such as the army, the navy, prisons, union workhouses, &c, and will comprise all such educational institutions as are supported either from the general taxes of the country or out of local rates.

And Wales. APPENDIX TO REPORT:— EXPLANATORY NOTES. 177

Some of these schools, however, will include among the scholars a certain number of *adults (i.e.* persons above twenty years of age), who must not be mixed up with scholars of the usual scholastic age.

If, therefore, the school is composed *entirely* of such adults, it must be wholly withdrawn from the tables; if partly of adults and partly of children, the number of the *children* only must be retained.

II. The second group is intended to embrace all schools distinctly designated in the returns as endowed, collegiate, and grammar schools; and, in addition, all schools, whatever may be their position or character in respect of the quality of the instruction given, which are supported, either altogether or in chief degree, by permanent *endowments.*

The principal means of determining what schools, besides those which are unmistakably described by their very title, should come within this definition, are supplied by the answers to the thirteenth question, as to the amount and sources of income. Where, in such cases, the reply concerning income is distinct and full, and it appears that part is derived from endowment and part from denominational subscriptions, the proportion Which the amount received from endowment bears towards the total income must be ascertained, and if this proportion should be found to exceed a half, the school must be referred to the present group; but if the proportion should be less than a half, and the receipts from voluntary contributions large, the school will most appropriately take its place with those of the third group. The great question will be, whether the endowment or the voluntary subscriptions form the *distinguishing feature* of the school j and according to the answer given to this inquiry will the school be placed in the second or the third division respectively.

The little inconvenience which might, perhaps, be apprehended from this plan, as one which mixes up in some degree together schools depending upon different

'kinds of support, will be effectually obviated by distinguishing, both in Class II. and Class III., the number of schools which are thus supported by a combination of endowments and subscriptions. But schools connected with philanthropic societies or institutions, such as orphan schools, blind schools, &c, should be placed in Class IV.

III. To the *Third* Group must be referred all Schools which are supported by Religious Denominations *as such;* and which, it may be presumed, are chiefly indebted for this support to the influence of a denominational spirit in their patrons.

The principal object of this Group is to separate all schools originated and sustained by denominational effort from those which are the result of a general philanthropy not flowing through the channel of any particular sect. This separation is essential to an accurate estimate of the extent to which the educational provision of the country is supplied by the operations of religious bodies. It is difficult, however, to find a perfect test by which this necessary division shall be satisfactorily secured. The best, perhaps, is furnished by the answer, given in the Returns, to Question 6., vie. "*With what, if any, Religious Denomination is* "*the School more particularly connected f*"; although—as the reply to this inquiry will, not infrequently, refer to the *form of religious instruction imparted* in the school, and as the present classification is intended to be framed according to the distinctive religious tenets of the *supporters* of the schools and not according to any distinctive religious tenets which may be *taught* in the schools—the invariable adoption of this test will not be proper; for it is evident that several schools which may, as far as peculiarities of *teaching* are concerned, be connected with particular religious bodies, ought nevertheless to be excluded from this group. Examples of such cases are presented by the School of the St Anne's Society at Brixton and the Orphan Working School at Haverstock Hill j both of which Institutions may be fairly assumed to be the offspring rather of philanthropic sentiment than of religious fieal—although the children of the former are instructed in the doctrines, though not receiving any sectarian instruction, are required to attend a Place f of Worship connected with Protestant Dissenters. In the same position are nearly all similar schools adapted for peculiar classes of children— such as schools for Orphans, for the Blind, for the Deaf and Dumb, for the children of Sailors, for Ragged Children, &c.:—most of these institutions being probably indebted for their origin, more to the promptings of a natural benevolence than to any denominational energy.

So, in the oase of schools maintained, directly or mediately, by the State, (forming Group I.); such as Military and Naval Schools, Prison Schools, and Workhouse Schools: although the scholars in such schools are generally instructed in the forms and doctrines of the Church of England, it cannot be maintained that these establishments belong to the National Church *as the source of their support.*

In like manner, schools supported principally by endowments—even although the donors may have been connected with particular denominations, and although particular creeds and catechisms may at present be imparted to the scholars— must nevertheless be excluded from a group designed to indicate the action of *existing* religious bodies in the eduoation of the people.

The safest course will probably be—in the case of all schools not established by 'the Government nor supported chiefly by endowments—generally to accept the answer to Question 6. (when mentioning particular religious bodies) as indicating a distinct denominational action, unless, from other portions of the Return under examination, it appears that the School is either adapted for a certain *class* of children specially claiming public sympathy (as those alluded to above) or connected with some secular institution or association (as Mechanics' Institution Schools, the Philanthropic Society's Farm School, &c.) or otherwise obviously founded and sustained by efforts not exclusively proceeding from any particular section of the religious world.

Where no reply at all is given to Question 6, or where the answer is to the effect that the School is not connected with any particular religious body; the school must be referred to the Fourth, or Miscellaneous Group, unless, from the name and description of the School, or from other information concerning it, there appears sufficient reason to assign to it a place in the present class. *British* schools had better be always included in Class DX; ascribing them to particular denominations, or to none, according to the answer given to Question 6.

Considerable light may be expected from the general language and incidental allusions of the Returns, which should therefore undergo a careful scrutiny for any hints they may afford upon this point IV. The *Fourth* Group will include all Public Schools, of whatever character, which cannot be referred to either of the preceding groups; and will chiefly consist of Schools connected with Public Secular Bodies—Charitable Institutions—or Philanthropic Associations—and those supported by benevolent individuals or bodies of subscribers actuated probably, in greatest measure, by religious principle, but not attached to any definite denominational machinery. Under this head will therefore appear all *Sagged* Schools, *Factory* Schools, and such other Schools as are not reported to belong to any particular Religious Body.

LONDON:
Printed by George E. Eyke and *William* Spottiswoodb, Printers to the Queen's most Excellent Majesty.

1